With the compliments
of the Canada Council

Avec les hommages
du Conseil des Arts
du Canada

Cross/cut

Cross/cut

Contemporary
English Quebec Poetry

Edited by

Peter Van Toorn & Ken Norris

Véhicule Press

Montréal, Canada

Published with the assistance of the Canada Council.
Cover artwork by Freda Guttman Bain entitled 'Writing on the Water'.
Cover graphics by JW Stewart.
Book design by Simon Dardick.

Special thanks to Intermedia Press, Anne McLean, Nancy Marrelli and the people at Cusaset.

Canadian Cataloguing in Publishing Data
Main entry under title:
Cross/cut: contemporary English Quebec poetry
Poems.
Bibliography: p.
ISBN: 0-919890-38-5 (bound). — ISBN: 0-919890-39-3 (pbk)
1. Canadian poetry (English)   — Quebec (Province)*
2. Canadian poetry (English)   — 20th century.*
I. Van Toorn, Peter, 1944-   II. Norris, Ken, 1951-
PS8295.5Q8C76   C811'.54'0809714   C82-090132-6
PR9195.7.C76

Véhicule Press, P.O.B. 125, Station "La Cité", Montreal, Canada H2W 2M9
Printed in Canada

This book is lovingly dedicated
to the memory
of A.M. Klein and John Glassco

Preface

This volume presents a survey of Quebec Anglophone poetic activity cresting in the late nineteen seventies and early eighties. It contains a representative selection of some seventy poets active during this period.

The editors regret omissions due to oversight or remoteness of orbit, and also regret the considerations of space and chronology which preclude reprinting material from earlier selections of this kind. The reader so interested is reminded that the gesture to anthologies of contemporary English poetry from Quebec has a history. The decade began with David Solway's seminal *Four Montreal Poets* (Fredericton, 1973); continued with Michael Harris' public elaboration, *Poetry Readings: Ten Montreal Poets at the CEGEPs* (Montreal, 1975); grew exponentially with Endre Farkas and Ken Norris' controversial *Montreal English Poetry of the Seventies* (Montreal, 1977); and expires with this proportionately comprehensive one.

We wish to thank Endre Farkas, at whose invitation this project was begun, and Louis Dudek, whose commitment to the making of modern Canadian poetry, and encouragement of every generation of poets included in this selection, is charged with significance.

Although it may now be time for a different cycle, we hope this spontaneous local ritual will have served some public and poetic purpose.

P.V.T. & K.N.
Little Athens, Que.
January, 1982

Contents

Introduction

Gentlemen, there are too many of us. —Yeats

1

When Yeats opened his address to the Rhymers Club at the turn of the present century with the above remark, he may have been commenting acidly upon a hiatus in some members' social vision—suspicious, perhaps, of increasing material restrictions imposed on their swelling numbers—but he could not have been disparaging the main company. They were too hugely original and brilliant: Moore, AE, Morris—just for starters—or Johnson, Davidson, Dowson, Symons, and Beardsley (even Wilde; once). Two decades later, Yeats extended his circuit from Dublin to London. At that time Pound, Eliot, and Frost were there. London in 1914 might still have hosted a convention of brilliant delegates from the arts, but they hailed from small ravaged areas. Most of England's literary resources were from the outlying colonies, principally Ireland, Scotland, and Wales. If we add to the list cited the names of Shaw, Synge, O'Casey, Joyce, Becket, and others in anticipation (such as Thomas and McDiarmid), we obtain a depressing picture of intense imaginative activity imported from areas characterized by political and economical squalor. Perhaps there is something inflammatory about the disclosure of statistics in a literary discussion; perhaps poets, anthologists anyway, tend to be too extravagant in their claims. This anthologist, for instance, presumes in cooperation with another to survey some of the most significant poetry to appear in the English speaking world in recent decades—in Québec, Canada. In consideration of the demography of English speaking people, this claim to significance on the part of a gypsy Anglophone group seems extravagant—there are over three hundred and fifty million English speaking people east, west, and south of Québec, but only half a million *in* Québec, and those mainly in its harbour metropolis, Montreal.

2

That so many poets exiled from their native home in the clouds to an area which historians envisage as a colony within a colony have such variety to offer within the brief span of a decade is impressive. The energy, abundance, and scope of their productions, within the last half dozen years especially, suggest that usufruct may no longer be an issue in Québec now that a change in consciousness is struggling to articulate itself in a mode of expression whose very subject is consciousness itself. At once a philosophical and historical mode, poetry refines our most public and private—and, therefore, our most elusive—currency. When it succeeds in providing a symbolic form for significant states of mind, poetry restores a balance and radiance not only to language, our spiritual currency, but to the imagination in charge of it, the human spirit invested with the awesome task of employing that currency with dignity. So in one sense, poetry is a beautiful worm with its head and tail in its middle—the place of the heart—where things are cut, healed, and made new. Poetry, therefore, is a redemptive mode whose lyric rhythms aspire to reach into primitive and civilized areas of consciousness simultaneously, especially at times of change or upheaval, in order to surface as a dramatic celebration of sacred intervals of space and time, between the airports and the stars, and between the ruby vibrations of men, women, and children of all nations. Perhaps that is why its genuine representatives have been described by one poet and critic (Ezra Pound) as the 'antennae of the race'.

Prophecies are never only of their own time and people, of course, but of all time and people, so it is not surprising that prophets have usually been to some degree exiled from their native home in the clouds. Many poets have transcended the temporal order during periods of social and political upheaval; many have succumbed to its distractions. Yet when the hoped-for change in consciousness establishes itself and the confusion settles, works embodying an imaginative synthesis will be discovered, much to the delight of the mind burdened by the imbalance which social conflict engenders, because the mind craves art. And the mind craves art because the mind is a work of art. Specimens of such poetic achievement can occur at any time, and although periods of intense change and distress may even contribute to their conception, they are more likely to achieve an imaginative radiance in epochs exuding peace and ease. During just such an epoch, the second half of the seventies, which fluctuated between points of intense change and stress and points of relaxation and ease, Canada witnessed a renewed flow of poetic energy. That these brief stretches of respite resembled a dotted line to which so many Canadian poets affixed their poetic signatures is a coincidence worth noting.

The flow experienced by poets in Québec, moreover, was not prim or neatly channelled. The variety, abundance, and intensity of their activity may reflect a cultural phenomenon, namely, that 'La Belle Province' periodically fosters more poets, certainly more of the authentic and indigenous ones—French and English—than the rest of Canada combined. Naturally, Québec's predominantly French speaking population is more warmly appreciative of its 'native' poets than of those included in this selection. An edition of poems by an original Québecois poet is sold out within months in Québec; a collection by a figure with popular stature, such as Gilles Vigneault, achieves the same result with a first run of ten thousand copies. Even the endorsement of Canada's most conspicuous literary prize, the Governor General's award, cannot attract half that many readers from all the provinces of Canada for an English book of poems. This situation has not altered profoundly since the precedent set by Lampman in 1895 when he finally found a publisher for his second volume in Boston through the efforts of his influential friend, Thomson: *Lyrics of Earth* appeared, after being rejected in both Canada and the States, in an edition full of blunders. Canada fosters many more poets now, of course, than it did in Lampman's time, hundreds more—of minor and major stature—but to the same degree of wholeheartedness. So it may be that Canada is still waiting for its poet. The obverse is true for Québec. Here is a description by Réjean Ducharme, in an article called 'Le Nez Qui Voque,' of a Québecois poet already famous at the turn of the century, who adopted the culture and language of his pianist Québecois mother instead of his Irish father:

> Chateaugué le trouve beau, dit qu'il a les cheveux comme en feu, un nez de lion et les yeux doux comme des ailes de papillon. La photo que nous avons volée le représente avec un lavallière autour du cou. La photo aurait pu la representer avec un lavallière autour du front. Alors, il aurait eu l'air arable. Les cheveux ardents, les yeux de femme, un nez de bête, les lèvres douces, la bouche dure; il est tout à fait comme nous nous l'imaginions: c'est cela qui nous a le plus frappés quand nous l'avons rencontré entre deux pages...

These are lover's terms, describing the Québecois poet Emile Nelligan.

The gypsy group of Canadian poets represented here, therefore, are at a serious disadvantage: for while they contribute significantly to Canadian literature, they enjoy the congenial reception of neither Canada nor Québec. This alienated position becomes more grievous when it is considered that Québec's poets constitute not only the bulwark of Canadian poetry (for up till recently Canadian poets from Quebec, whether Québecois or English, accounted for eighty percent of the contents in major anthologies) but that they also constitute, along with the novelists of Québec, the main body of writers who effect the translating of Québec's imaginative contours. From a serious point of view, these observations about poetic currents based on sales figures are subject to dispute and proclaim little more than the indices of popular vagary, the market's response to what's in fashion. A further objection to these observations could be made. Excellence has always involved more hard work than Utopians allow for. And it may be that Québec's indigenous population feels inclined to dreaming. Encumbered by its Cartesian heritage—its predilection for metaphysical introspection, revolutionary reform, egalitarian fervour, love of *pays*, and consuming passion for political debate—Québec is, moreover, out of touch with an English host who is saddled with foreign traditions—with British empiricism in science and philosophy, and with American pragmatism in commerce and politics. Nevertheless, Québec has provided the concerted support needed to elect the party and prime minister piloting Canada through its difficult passage to nationhood in the seventies and early eighties. So from a visionary perspective (and it is the visionary perspective with which we are concerned here, the sympathies and reflections which guide us into the future and past simultaneously, and which make our present source resonate with unity and clarity, not sad separateness or violent opposition), the renascence of poetic life across Canada, if that phrase does not exaggerate the phenomenon of recent small press activity, indicates that something besides oil is being found: namely, that the identities of Canada and Québec are simultaneously undergoing radical metamorphosis.

3

Québec's role in Canada's evolution has been largely heuristic. Its capacity for 'negative capability' (to stretch Keats' definition of poetic capacity a little and apply it more generally to the creative mood in politics and economics) is not well understood. If Québec's participation in the economic sphere of Canada has been limited, its influence on policies affecting the imaginative dimensions and directions of Canada has been as inspirational and decisive as the silence and desultory eruptions of Canada's aboriginals. By its mere presence, Québec has positioned the visionary template of Canada, on which Canadians count and build. Perhaps in this respect Québec's traditional heritage, although once considered its weakness, has really proved to be its strength. (Mark Twain is reported as having made a crack about Québec's traditional loyalty to the church. During his visit to Montreal, a city which has retained much of its old architecture despite the rapid growth of skyscrapers and industry in the past two decades, Twain remarked: 'Montreal is the only city in North America where you can't throw a brick without breaking a church window.') A capacity for enlightened endurance, vivacious celebration, and irreverence assists a people in facing long, snowbound winters: it assuages irritation and dispels the proclivity to scepticism and mortification which a society imbued with predominantly Catholic and agrarian values feels when making the transition to a predominantly industrial and Protestant way of life, especially those segments of the population for whom such a radical transition entails massive urbanization. Take away Québec's tendency to fervent introspection and its subsequent aspiration to political autonomy, and it resembles its stoic neighbour to the south, New England.

Sometimes in indigence, sometimes in brusque self assertion, sometimes in quest of a discrete spiritual synthesis, Québec has endeavoured to embody a conception of existence which stands in stark contrast to the dominant mode of industrial and mercantile efficiency characteristic of the more North American style of operation. Québec's Anglophones have had some role in the shaping of this new mode of existence, especially those who have stimulated a vision of man as the measure of all things—'La personne avant toutes choses'—a vision which Canada's political institutions accommodate with increasing accuracy and élan. Thus, by its imaginative contrast, its silence as well as its unique philosophical development, Québec has contributed something precious to the Canadian identity. If this contribution has been gradual, inspissatory, and unacknowledged, Québec remonstrates Canada for the degree to which the latter has still to diffuse a block in its imaginative flow: paradoxically, the way Canada treats Québec reflects the way it treats its aborigines, its origins, and itself.

The recent drive for independence issuing from Québec is paradoxically a renewed invitation to Canada, a way of inviting it to reinterpret its history. To reinterpret the history of Canada means to reinterpret the original settling motives and to reinterpret the history of Europe and the States *vis-à-vis* Canadian history. Although this invitation has all the clamour of an infant struggling for nourishment and growth, it is a cordial one, with all the promise of dividends which the metaphor implies. And it is an urgent invitation to revision, for if Canada is to avoid the species of civil strife which has erupted in the United States from time to time, it must revise its conception of origins and original purposes, about which the States and Europe have brooded and struggled much longer. In a sense, Québec's remonstrative behaviour is an appeal to Canada's historical conscience. Canada has still to revise its conception of a viable democracy. To accept or emulate solutions the United States has stumbled on is to accept American history instead of creating a Canadian one; to accept a foreign solution is to stay under a foreign thumb. If Canada accepts Québec's cordial invitation to a symposium on the subject, with intentions to act on its findings and, more importantly, with intentions of sharing in decision making, it will begin to consider the implications of policies which at present oppress a third of its population conveniently concentrated in a small area of its enormous domains. These policies, which are both cultural and economical, are policies which Canada has not created in full consciousness but which it passively accepted for itself. These are policies which are restrictive rather than expansive; they discourage rather than initiate self motivation, and they attempt sporadically to relieve symptoms rather than consistently and respectfully deal with their causes.

To such policies Québec's only option until recently has been cultural genocide or radical Anglicization. That these policies are colonial, that they are historically myopic, that they are congestive rather than carminative is obvious. That such policies do not enucleate the favourable sense which Aesop and Keats decree they might in their aphorisms, 'A good deed lives forever,' and 'A thing of beauty is a joy forever'—that such policies contain seeds which will, in the future, be a cause of embarrassment or rue—is not so obvious. The dilemma invokes the Muse.

4

Three areas of endeavour in which Québec has supplied Canada a model for a novel and imaginative approach to itself are aesthetic philosophy, political debate, and social consciousness. The first needs no elaboration. (Figures who illustrate the application of aesthetic principles to several areas of our life are numerous—from Nelligan to Vigneault, from Trudeau to Lafleur.) It is only logical that Québec should be keenly interested in contributing to the second area of endeavour. Québec inherits from its founders and cultural antecedents a passion for political debate with a revolutionary orientation. From its humanist tradition, from the *savants* and founders of the Enlightenment down to the existentialist *philosophes* of recent times, Québec inherits a faculty for rational analysis and introspection (annoying as that faculty may be when it ministers to an obsession with classification). Québec inherits from its language, moreover, an instrument of extraordinary precision and subtlety, tailored by the Académie Française through the centuries for the purpose of exploring what Pascal termed *la raison du coeur*. To this sensitive tongue, capable of expressing subtle nuances of feeling, Québec has contributed its own rhythms and vocabulary. Québec has restored to French some of its original Medieval vibrancy: the intestinal twang and scouring plangency of Villon surfaces in contemporary Québecois, which at its best is richly demotic, with a jazzy scat patter whose Anglicisms are a sad but comic parody of the current attitude which outsiders hold to the French tongue. Finally, from its legal matrix, from its Code Napoléon, and from its experience of subjugation, Québec has come to be imbued with a resilience to the numerical, military, and economic superiority of its English neighbours. In response to these historical experiences, Québec has developed not only an aspiration to autonomy but a unique twist of flavour for debate. For whatever it has contributed to the debate of Canada's identity and the configuration of its democratic ideals, Québec has, by its insistence on self parody and on the repudiation of colony status, for itself as well as for all Canadians, infused Canada's parliamentary style with panache.

The third area in which Québec has provided a model for a novel and imaginative approach to Canadian history is social consciousness, the very fabric out of which some kind of poetry is made. Comments on this aspect must be limited and brief; a fuller exploration of the substance and value of Québec's social consciousness should be made by a ripe Québecer. Let it be said, however, that Québec's 'rainbow vision' of society, its cultural catholicity, its ethnic pluralism, is difficult to understand. Why, for example, should Québec, struggling for its own survival as an ethnic group, exhibit a cordial welcome to a confluence of alien groups—the people immigrating from the States, Europe, the U.K., Asia, South America, the Middle and Far East, and from other parts of Canada? One possible explanation is that Québecers extend their hospitality to small groups from other parts of the globe because most immigrants tend, or have tended, until recently to flow into English life and so they do not strain the economic or psychic tolerance of the Québecois (that is, in any way oppose Québec's aspiration to freedom, being too preoccupied with their own survival and acculturization). Other explanations may be tried. But whether the cosmopolitan mosaic of Québec, Montreal's pluralist mosaic especially, owes its existence to an enlightened Protestant English minority or to a charitable Catholic French majority is difficult to determine. Ethnic and cultural pluralism, however, seems more conspicuously vital in Québec than elsewhere in Canada. So perhaps Québec's enlightened social consciousness is more developed than has been supposed.

5

If the preceding remarks err on the side of truth, it follows that the much debated topic of Canada's identity has a great deal in common with the endemic political fermentation and the aspiration to independence issuing from Québec. Perhaps it is, or has been, Québec's directives to secession that have roused the provinces horizontally, for economically the vertical pull to the States appears more compelling. Given Québec's increasingly articulate provocations, Canada has become more imaginatively agonized over its unity and direction: it has started to repudiate its image of itself as an attic of the United States and as an unrepatriated colony of England. It has proceeded to accept a mode of becoming at the pace of a native Indian dithyramb and dilated its 'democratic vistas' proportionately.

Historians might reasonably argue that assigning Québec a major role in the drama of Canadian maturation is a fond but foolish judgement. They would probably aver that an interpretation of the causes behind any renewal in self confidence, any renascence in the Canadian vision, which did not focus on economic issues, and largely on American ones, would be simplistic. And they could muster a number of events, and the absence of events, to support a more pragmatic point of view. They might claim that Canada's relative freedom from involvement in any international crisis since the last world war has left it with energy to devote to domestic affairs; or that, rather than any resurgence of separatism, the influx of American idealism in protest of the war in Vietnam supplied Canada with extra confidence and heightened its momentum in the seventies. But an indigenous Québecois poetry, one that does not consciously strive to emulate an American or European poetics, or to find acclaim outside of Québec, does not seem to bear this inference out.

6

What such an indigenous Québecois poetry (as distinct from a colonial or derivative poetry) does seem to bear out is a commitment to becoming adjusted to origins. This commitment to locating a source, an original starting point, a free slate, redeemed from history, is a commitment to a particular experience, one of defeat, resignation, containment, endurance, ascesis, and faith rooted in social vision. This attention to origins, to an authentic point of arrival, is also an attention to final things, to a radiant point of departure. Such an apocalyptic attention must arrange itself in metaphors of becoming to match the unconscious ambivalence of the Canadian imagination to history itself. The Canadian imagination is confused about its origins, which lie about in another time and space, either entangled in the historv of Western civilization, European civilization in particular, or buried alive in the Canadian past, in the encounter with Canada's original inhabitants, its Inuit and Indian aboriginals, and later, in its encounter with the French settlers. Much of the European stuff is not actively part of most Canadians' cultural apparatus; much of the Canadian past isn't either, consisting of obscure records of violence, of a series of conquests rather than original discoveries. Wherever the historical record depicts a contact made with authentic origins—the paintings of Emily Carr, for example, whose contact with the lustral realm of the West Coast Indians registers an unmistakeable shock of discovery, by a European on a spiritually equal footing with her aboriginal neighbours—the artistic result has been rich and impressive. This tradition of the *voyage* is an eminently French tradition (Carr and some of the Group of Seven painters started developing only after returning from France, fresh from their discovery of Impressionism), and accounts of this spiritual *voyage* are to be found in the *Essaies* of Montaigne as well as in the *Journal* of Saint-Denys-Garneau, they are to be found in the poems of Rimbaud, who prescribed a program for himself which involved 'the derangement of all the senses' (*le poète se fait 'voyant' par un long, immense et raisonné dérèglement de tous les sens*) and a conviction in the belief of the poet as *voyant*, seer; similar records of authentic contact with an indigenous Canadian imagination are to be found in the paintings of Tom Thomson, whose lonely searching in the North led to the first imaginative use of oil.

That Québecois poetry exhibits a peculiar mode of assimilating experience, one which focusses its attention on origins and arranges its findings in metaphors of becoming, is not surprising. Insofar as Québecois poetry is not resigned, it is a poetry of high achievement. The Québecois have, after all, settled in one place; they have, like the aboriginals on their reservations, chosen a spiritual rather than a secular expansion. Their poetry shows it: it is marked by a tendency to manifest containment, introspection, declaration, evocation, meditation, transformation, and celebration with central figures of Christian suffering as protagonists, comic as well as earthy. True, the commitment of the Québecois to origins and to authentic vision has been made for them as well as by them. Their commitment is a redemptive one, less clearly stained by the blood of conquest, the lurching rhythms of imperial expansion, the violent confrontations which epitomize the drama of frontier consciousness. Thomas Gray's 'Elegy', said to have been recited by Wolfe on the eve of the fateful battle, contains two cautionary lines which apply to the Québecois in their commitment: 'nor circumscribed alone. Their growing virtues, but their crimes confined....' Nevertheless, much Québecois artistic endeavour has the flavour of original discovery rather than of conquest. In short, Québec has provided the ambience in which a new consciousness might develop.

7

Québec has thus nourished a Canadian poetry into a youthful identity of its own. Canadian poets have experienced this stance partly by choice, by choosing to remain in Québec rather than adopt a more established literary centre, and partly by luck, by finding themselves immersed in a French cultural framework and by absorbing the aspirations and achievements of the French imagination in literature and philosophy in the past and present. Even poets born and raised in other parts of Canada, the United States, and elsewhere, when they have experienced some of their crucially formative years in Québec, have subsequently imaginatively identified their experience of Québec with the impulse to artistic autonomy, decolonization, and to originality—to reaching more deeply into their own roots upon returning to their adopted region or native home. Much of what they made of Québec and its experience, much of what subsequently informed their imaginative commitment, had to do with the fact that an accelerated dispossession of ethnic pluralism was not mandatory in Québec as elsewhere. Whether you were from Paris, St. Johns, Calgary, Athens, Melbourne, Bombay, Tokyo, San Francisco, Prague, or Amsterdam, in Montreal you were at home.

8

If one wishes to know what it has meant to be a poet in Canada until recently, whether in or out of Québec or for that matter, what it has meant to be a visionary in Canada in any role, one has only to remember that Lampman died after finally finding a reluctant publisher for his work through a New York agent—and Lampman was one of Canada's first, and still one of its finest; that Klein abruptly curtailed his meteoric career with twenty years of silence; that Nelligan suffered a premature abrogation of sanity and a lapse into more than forty years of silence; and that Saint-Denys-Garneau exposed himself increasingly to a metaphysical mortification which would frighten a Carmelite monk. Each of these poets ended life in a terrible isolation whose cause is not to be conveniently extrapolated from the facts of biography by some fashionable paradigm from sociology, psychology, or economics: for each of these poets was crushed in his imaginative hopes and poetic endeavours by the relentless inertia of historical progress. The price of their vision was dereliction, not economic and social, but imaginative dereliction.

There is something about imaginative dereliction, if we are familiar with the lives of artists such as Smart, Baudelaire, and Van Gogh, which suggests that their madness was the kind which society, had it had the perspicacity and enlightened self-interest to cherish these artists before their demise, could have drawn strength from, namely the apocalyptic sanity which it sadly lacked—our continued devotion to these artists is proof of that. Lampman, to return to a Canadian artist of this stamp, died inwardly of stultification long before he contracted the heart ailment that led to his death. Like some coco-chewing mountain porter of the Andes, squeezed out of the more congenial, temperate valleys by the aggressively mercantile Spanish hacienda elite, Lampman had no alternative. There was probably no escape for him into a world more congenial to the imagination. Such a world did not exist in Canada at the time, if it ever did, anywhere, except, perhaps, for brief accidental moments, and where least expected: Emily Carr looked for it later in the rainforests of the West Coast Indians. And Canada has had to pay for its colonial folly: for if an artist cannot altogether escape the conditions of his own time except at moments of creation, it is equally true that men and women collectively cannot escape them at all when they are deaf to the imaginative exertions around them. So if Lampman suffers the conditions of colonialism in his less favourable productions, but transforms them, or transcends them, in his best, then the imaginative conditions of society must have been very indigent generally. Take a look at the price of colonialism in his work. In his best work, and that usually meagerly anthologized—there is currently almost a Canadian embarrassment about Lampman in vogue—he is finding a uniquely personal and Canadian idiom, and working out of local landscapes and portraits toward a prophetic vision, of the sort we find in "Heat", his great Canadian pastoral lyric, with its intensely apocalyptic solar vision, its scientific objectivity, meditative ecstasy, and imagist congeniality.

His straining in the vein of *fin-de-siècle* hellenism, his emulation of classical subjects and models, or his imitation of the then popular strokes of transcendentalist fatuity by Carman at his worst, are now all but unreadable. Like Tom Thomson, the painter, Lampman tried to escape his essentially colonial situation almost physically; like Thomson (or Rimbaud, whose ascetic travels and feats of physical endurance Enid

Starkie describes in her vivid account of the French *voyant*, Lampman travelled back into a spiritually vital, emblematic, neglected area of our consciousness, into the terrain buried under the abstraction of dominion.

Neither Lampman nor Thomson wholly integrated the connection with mythic time in the bush and secular time in the community, indigenous and colonial time respectively. They were not able to integrate the consciousness which they were after and which they wanted to share imaginatively with us—to succeed in that aim they would have had to succeed in projecting a vision not only on an imaginative, artistic scale, but to succeed in living with it among people in a community; and such a community did not exist. Lampman and Thomson lived their visions in solitude and in art. Emily Carr, the painter, perhaps more than either of these two great Canadian artists, accomplished a blazing identification with an indigenous vision, the symbolic, totemic, lustral realm of the West Coast aboriginals. Both Thomson and Lampman were reclaimed by the wilderness: Lampman contracted a heart ailment during an over-strenuous hike (the ailment was further strained by the difficulties he experienced getting his second book of poems published), and Thomson died mysteriously, in a way that is legend by now. And if 'Nature never betrayed the heart that loved her,' then her reclamations were, hopefully, merciful.

But that part of our heritage which has been forgotten, overlooked, or insidiously repudiated—not a Romantic version of it by Drummond, Service, or Carman, but the real thing—still lies waiting. It is a door the immigrant in his deepest moments swings open. It is a vision of the unexpected. It is a vision of becoming. It is a vision, moreover, which the early governors of European courts intent on colonizing Canada could not find reference to in their mandates, and which leaders of the white race have been incapable of acculturating to. It is a vision which the Indians were in touch with, and which made them in turn fierce, and then, after their defeat and losses, sad and demoralized. The voyageurs may have kept a nomadic trace of it in their stream of consciousness; such a transmission would account for the residual difference in the vision issuing from Québec. But it is not a vision of man with a supernatural relation to man and nature, of man going in and out of sync with his awareness of the numinous—man as the measure of all things. And wherever this vision has been neglected by men driven against men and nature in a Faustian hurry, there is an incompleteness to be found. This incompleteness is one of the conditions which Wilgar, in his classic essay, 'The Divided Mind,' claims as the cause for the lack of any truly first-rate Canadian poetry.

Sometimes a Québec poet, a poet having passed through the

experience of which Québec is a metaphor, hints hugely at this vision of Canada. Certain monumental, lyric, never totally achieved poems come to mind from the Canadian bestiary: Nowlan's 'The Bull Moose,' with its Christian archetype embedded in its pastoral Maritime matrix; Layton's 'The Bull Calf,' with its elegiac Marxism and funerary catharsis; and especially Acorn's lament for the cosmic circus, 'The Natural History of Elephants,' with its pan-Canadian gnosticism. To the degree which each of these poems laments the death of the poet, the Canadian imagination laments the loss of its aboriginal past. The loss of this vision is what Klein compassionately laments in his 'Portrait of the Poet as Landscape,' and which he invokes in his 'Montreal'. The abeyance of this vision within Canada's institutions is a discovery which Atwood too makes in her sardonic 'The Landlady' poem. This vision includes a world which Purdy bravely assembles in his unique selection of Canadian poetry, *Fifteen Winds;* which Cohen evokes in his warm collection of lyrics, *The Spice Box of Earth*; which Lee commemorates in his *Civil Elegies;* and which Pratt parodies into possibility against the rollicking pageant of a mechanistic cosmos. There are huge, warm doses of it in the plum blossom poems of Souster, in the scientifically observed ecstasies of Lampman, and in the poems of several other Canadian poets. But generally this vision is rendered with a more local and certain passion by Québecois poets.

In the last decade a change in stance on the part of Canadian poets to this incompleteness of the Canadian imagination has become more evident. There are still no Canadian happenings like the Québecois 'La Nuit de Poésie,' but there has grown a kind of deeper, sometimes aggressively obsessive, preoccupation with Canadian identity, resulting in the attempt to shake off vestiges of colonial conditions. The recent reluctance to reach out to creative influences from outside, whether from the States, Europe, Asia, or Russia (the reluctance diminishes when its scope approaches third world countries) stems from a distaste for the Faustian thrust of the European Enlightenment. A look for something here and now, a kind of antidote to the perpetual threat of holocaust, is what Jones and Layton posit as the central preoccupation of the younger poets. A brief digression on the technical features which this approach appears to entail for most Canadian poets may be useful. Three features (paraphrased from an excellent essay by Paul West) seem to dominate contemporary Canadian poetry: 1) a one-side-of-a-pinetree look, a ragged stichic mode of verse assimilation; 2) a tendency to a discursive, rapidly discontinuous epic of daily life; 3) and an aspiration to vocal imagism, the verbal representation of the shape of sound. And these technical characteristics appear not so much in a satiric vein, for we have produced little satire of great permanence (unless Scott's and Smith's anthology of satire, *The Blasted Pine*, argues otherwise), not so much in satiric, as in elegiac form. The loon crowds out our best moments.

9

   If current poetry from Québec, Francophone especially, but Anglophone as well, shows less tendency to emulate the trends of foreign literary movements, and despite whatever loss in artistic possibility this hermetic stance may entail, whatever it does emulate or reflect is not a Québec as it has conventionally been viewed by outsiders, but a human condition for which Québec has provided a working political metaphor: a motion of becoming. This 'hermeneutic motion' (Steiner's phrase for the process of all translation) is a fragile mode of growth, as fragile as the grip which the flora and fauna of the Arctic have upon life during their brief summer existence, yet entirely appropriate to Canada. And if Québec, in its slow ascension, reverses the spiritual tailspin which characterizes the fate of Canada's most completely indigenous peoples, its Inuit and Indians, it has certainly exhibited an easy tolerance for the pluralist society which has constituted the buffer between the traditionally Cartesian way of Québecois life, with its rigours, mortifications, and assertions of political belief, and between the way of life prevalent on all sides. Québec's tolerance for a plurality of values, despite some few recent signs of xenophobia, is not easy to grasp. In the compulsive and acquisitive traffic towards an abstract state of well being which appears to be the consuming goal of a half hearted democracy, the small and the politically weak are often ignored. But Québec, with a shrug of the shoulders, has adopted a confluence of native and alien civilizations: it has been a sanctuary and a watershed for the refugees and the dispossessed seeking inner clarification, in Cohen's phrase, via 'all the languages of Montreal.' It has provided this hospitality and asylum in a spirit free of condescension, and in a mood of increasing independence from what Frye has called 'the garrison mentality' that a protracted colonialism settled in Canada's imaginative life, whether in poetry or in politics.

   That the search for Canadian identity, a quest which, for better or worse, now informs the somewhat nationalist movement of the Canadian literary scene, is further advanced in Québec is not surprising; that this momentum is readily converted into a specific economic metaphor outside of Québec is a feature of our empiricism. The history of English poetry, science, and philosophy is to some degree a history of unacknowledged appropriation from extraneous sources, especially French ones. England's application of the French Revolution is a case in point. England was the first to industrialize and establish colonies in various continents after it investigated the positive scientific and philosophic method developed in France. America followed suit. And their language served them well. English borrows easily, and more readily from French because of their common classical heritage. But it refuses—and this refusal, which extends into American and Canadian history in different forms, is paradoxically a logical feature of empiricism—to express a debt of gratitude in any terms which would help resolve the tension we now find ourselves in. As Canada has begun to crystalize in response to Québec's rigorous introspection and subsequent metamorphosis, successive generations of Canadian poets in Québec have endeavoured to mediate the gap. Where Québec has provided the atmosphere of integrity, the unique aesthetic philosophy, and the political motivation to enshrine a new conception of man, various Québecois ethnic writers have supplied the creative *élan vital.*

10

The revamping of colonial attitudes in art represents the catabolic phase in the chemistry of the Canadian vision; it indicates what artists and thinkers in the Nuclear Era have been trying not to do. Their repudiation has come to mean trying to be at home in the wilderness, not of trees, though that too, but of faces, varieties of speech, sensibility, ways of being—at home with historic pluralism, with a global specimen of humanity threatened, in the face of plenty, by the chaos resulting from a desire to impose a political identity derived from past models on what is a state of natural flux. Québec is a small community, smaller in population than many communities which occupy a tenth of its area, a community, moreover, which is still trying to find itself in a situation of bewildering complexity caused by its having to assimilate the confluence of radically diverse values and histories, while having to confront the blandishments of the most industrialized and competitive nations in the world. Québec is much in difficulty. But it is exceptionally brave and witty in its view of its giant neighbours. Québec has, of course, no experience with the consequences of nationalism and fascism, since it participated very little in the disasters which Canadians and Americans confronted in Europe; and Québec's ingenuousness may cause it much distress in the future. But insofar as it has asserted itself in bringing about a new state of societal being, a new, richer, more democratic life, Québec has demonstrated something valuably Canadian.

The Anglophone poet remaining in Québec is just as witty as the Québecois poet, in at least one sense, for he now faces what Québec has long faced, but he faces it entirely alone. Sensitive to the wastefulness of conflict, even a little envious of his Québecois counterpart's more congenial environment, and despite all the affection and sympathy he feels for the new Québec (and doubts, reservations, fears, and antipathies too), the Anglophone poet now finds himself in a situation which was evident all along, but which he closed his eyes to: cultural dereliction. For his community, language, and identity have abandoned him. The fate of dereliction is implicit in the situation: a fragile mode of becoming surrenders to laws other than those which the parties of empiricism and rationalism engage in. His marginal status was never very secure, as Klein in his 'Portrait of the Poet as Landscape' sadly points out, and which the lives of Nelligan, Saint-Denys-Garneau, Klein, Lampman, and Thomson illustrate. But the erosion of even his marginal status now brings up the spectre of exile on an imaginative scale.

Up to very recently the Anglophone poet rooted in Québec was able to observe with imaginative perspicacity the hopes, aspirations, and struggles for self determination of the Québecois and its minorities: he was able to accomplish this much commitment by immersing himself in all the cultures and by contributing to a vision of Québec and Canada simultaneously. His very pluralist identity, his passionate complexity, and his detachment from merely political solutions were in themselves a source of strength and insight. The sometimes bohemian ambiance, even intolerant arrogance, when it did not polarize into mordant trenchancy and terrorism, was amniotic and propulsive: it fostered a metaphor of becoming.

Now a new vision, if that term is appropriate to a description of recent events, is being increasingly shaped by the conflicting groups whose positions will for some time isolate the poet. For the heat of the debate will assure each side of an increasing resemblance, without room for the diversity which lubricated the once visionary *élan*. That is the fate of historical conflict: we become what we unthoughtfully reject, fail for too long to try to understand, or exploit for profane ends. So that amazing period of flux, of hovering at the brink of a vision of man, is about to be embodied or rejected in Québec. To the *poète Anglais* (a term which must sound faintly risible to the *poète Québecois*) the numinous period of transition, of vibrant trance, for better or worse, is over. Dreams are becoming responsibilities. The enormous potential of what the poet has always dreamed of must now slip out of his being into the hands of those who claim to be more practical.

11

In a purely literary context, it seems inevitable that a poet from an area such as Québec, containing several dozen peoples attempting mutual translation, should adopt a more densely textured vernacular than has been common for a poetic medium. Such a philosophic and linguistic strain seems implicit in the practice of a poet working the grain of his native speech against the rhythms and perspectives of two kinds of English, two kinds of French, and the *mélange* of sonorities provided by dozens of European, Asian, and Eastern tongues. The fusion of French and English sensibilities in particular, has been one of the concerns of English poetry for seven centuries. D'Orleans, after all, wrote fluently in both languages and is represented in the anthologies of English and French speaking peoples. An interest in French civilization has been a characteristic of writers as diverse as Dostoyevski, Goethe, Wordsworth, and Pien Chih-Lin. In Québec, this same interest in French civilization has been extended to include an interest in contempory Québecois literature. This interest has long been manifested by poets and translators such as Dudek, Klein, Scott, Smith, Jones, and Glassco; some of the younger poets included in this selection, such as Brockwell, Harris, Plourde, McGee, and Filip are continuing the patterns set by their seniors.

The reasons for the interest which English writers exhibit in French literature, its poetry and critical prose especially, are obvious. English shares with French and the Romance languages a common classical heritage—the mythology, philosophy, science, and literature of Ancient Rome and Greece. Moreover, after the Norman invasion, the courts of England practised French language and general culture for centuries to come, a custom which became widely adopted throughout Europe. But the attraction that French civilization, its literature in particular, exercises upon English minds is best explained by the aphorism, *les extrèmes se touchent.* For there is a body of literature which the English mind finds necessary to its imaginative diet, but which it has to locate outside its own tradition, to locate it at all: this is the stream of gentle scepticism and radical introspection which is represented by a Montaigne, Pascal, Descartes, Baudelaire, Rimbaud, Nelligan, or Saint-Denys-Garneau. Rooted in religious dogma or secular revolt, this tradition of gentle scepticism and subtle introspection is never out of touch with the fluid humanism and resigned humour which epitomizes a Montaigne, the sublime pathos but austere devotion typical of a Saint-Denys-Garneau, the visionary rompings which radiate from the utterances of a Rimbaud, or the tender and exalting lyrics of a Vigneault. The tendency in English, American, and

Canadian literature, however, has been to investigate this tradition cautiously, and to react negatively to its findings—a tendency which sometimes betrays a degree of covert arrogation, for a steady empiricism and flexible pragmatism has been pervasive in the English enterprise since the Industrial Revolution. This tendency becomes clearer if the direction of Western technology and science is considered as the historic application of the principles of Judeo-Christian democracy in material form. From this perspective, modern capitalist democracy is partly the result of the French Revolution and of the principles emanating from the European Enlightenment.

English poets and critics have been signally reticent about their French sources (Arnold, Eliot, Pound, and, in this selection, Dudek, Glassco, Jones, and Scott are among the exceptions which prove the rule; that is, they are truly exceptions) because the majority have felt a need for insulation against the leavening influence which a study of French civilization induces. A bridge between French and English sensibilities involves more than the identity which Wallace Stevens claimed for them in his wily aphorism, 'French and English constitute one language.' Contact with French civilization involves contact with more than French values alone, if that contact is to be at least as inspired as French democratic ideals declare it should be. The goddess of Reason, like the angel of Liberty in New York Harbour, shines her lamp of freedom ubiquitously on the sombre mysticism of the Spanish; the dazzling fluidity of the Arabic and Moorish; the psychological subtlety of the French ironists mentioned earlier; the airy abandon and refinement of the Italian; the penchant for delicate reverie and truculent vituperation possessed by the Scots, Welsh, and Irish; the vitality and serpentine wisdom which the Greeks continue to manifest in their unifying myths and pastoral lamentations; the passion for justice, tender eroticism, and ironic empathy which illuminates the Jewish spirit; and the still largely esoteric principle of excluded middle (whose concomitants are moderately henothism, ritual incantation, and fluid osmosis) which Asian and Eastern philosophy and poetry evince, and which various intuitive forms such as yoga, zen, astrology, meditation, and the use of oracles have popularly applied to practical purposes such as the regulating and synchronizing of body and mind. These are a few of the patterns which a study of French civilization involve, and which will, in time to come, emblazon the pluralist mosaic of Canadian poetry.

12

That Québec's English writers, recently labouring in an ambiance of mass exodus, manifest signs of willingness to be influenced by these various strains, or to endeavour a voluntary incursion into the realms of visionary idiolect or private language, an aspiration which goes back to Klein's poetry and prose and to Saint-Denys-Garneau's poetry and philosophic investigations—suggests that something is stirring in Canada's literary climate. The synoptic task of determining its relevance to a wider imaginative context remains with the qualified critic. The pleasure of discovery, after all, remains the primary objective of a selection of contemporary poetry.

Peter Van Toorn
Montreal, June 1982

Mona Elaine Adilman

BILL 101

The language of De Musset,
La Rochefoucauld, Voltaire
anthologizes music
from a foreign sphere.

The nearer voices
of Saint-Denys-Garneau,
Hébert, Nelligan
haunt my reality
with shimmering texture,
and I reach out
in hunger, weave myself
into a rich fabric
I only partly understand.

The speech of Tremblay,
Vignault, Arsenault
cavorts on fiddle strings,
twangs a gut tune
of poignancy
and joie de vivre.

The French idiom
is a sparkling apéritif,
a savory, tongue-teasing
platter of hors d'oeuvres.
I gulp each delicacy
with voracity.

But my Mother-tongue
. . . English . . .
breathes from my pores,
runs radiant in my veins,
lines the creative womb
with pulsating words.

I inherit the resonance
of Shakespeare and Milton,
the luminous landscapes
of Keats and Shelley,
the fertile images
of Carlyle and Ruskin.

The past flows into me.
Benevolent centuries
monitor my aching pen,
strengthen philosophic wings.
My thoughts flower
in English.

In a linguistic universe
animated with galaxies
of speech, French is
a brethren language.

But English frees my mind,
unshackles the emotions,
drains frustrations,
tethers the soul
to the furthermost stars.

February 11, 1979

ICE PORTRAIT

Icicles tong my garden.
The choke-cherry tree
blooms crystal berries.

Hunched like a pensioner,
the honeysuckle hedge
hoards frosty coins.

Glacial fruits
sculpture a mosaic
of frozen light.

A mysterious
centigrade presence
creates glass rainbows.

I trespass on sunlight,
smudge transient footprints
on white linen snow.

A whisper of wind
unburdens the branches.
Eider down prisms

blizzard my shoulder,
perch like silver birds
on my singing fingertips.

Robert Allen

FETISHISTS

The world is so full of contradictions,
we are forced to fall back on the assumption
of private lives. So much of our hope

is self-translation, scintilla
of private planets kindled to a blaze.
In a house of my own, I eat the chill black

of a photographic plate,
an arctic of its own that is immaculate light.
I am tangled up in things, but won't let

the fetishist, with his arc-lights and his arctic
sense of size, shovel out the things in a poor man's shack,
as if his objects could ever amount to life.

THE NEWT'S SONG

A ripple of sadness passes through
the tough forearms of the newt,

the corners of his lidless eyes
pull with a shiver to close.

Summer falls sad
on the newt, & autumn drills deep

through his thin blood. Hardly known,
the rock cleft, the warm sun,

hardly known, the cold that hums
with swift harmonics, blown snow.

However many autumns: same, same, sings
the newt, that knows only one.

SKETCH ON SILK

This might be China
beyond the wall: its lick
of hill line, a single

or two strokes; sky
thus reined, no blue
but what's implied.

Snow all plane and contour,
A dozen birch, like a frozen leak
from a tin roof.

Lake sealed tight; further
hills, like a rumpled silk sleeve.

A fisherman
in parka and blue hood
lights a cold cigarette.

Brittle tobacco,
sulphur tugging at the lung;

quiet snarl of smoke,
silk scarf on the grey branch.

John Asfour

A LETTER

Let the universe come from your hand;
　　　Let it run.
Let the stars twinkle and tilt,
Draw them on the page,
　　　Make them burn.
Flush ink on the burning stars;
　　　Cool them.
Joggle them and change their places on the paper.
Make their edges touch.
Caress the light they produce.
　　　Stare at the magnitude,
For the stars have some magnitude left.
After you finish your drawings, your writings, your
　　　scribblings,
Fold the paper, fold the stars.
Listen to the sound of the paper.
Place it in an envelope
　　　And send it to me.

Brian Bartlett

IN A HOUSE WHERE CHASTITY
WAS TAUGHT FOR A CENTURY

In a house where chastity was taught for a century
a bastard son sleeps between his grandparents
in a bed hardly wide enough for two.
Ornamented with headboard horses, his crib
split last night under his kicking.
Now his mother's blossom scent is fainter
than the musk of the hound on the rug.

By this pale hour in the nearest town
she has left her walls of bright posters.
Gas-station girl, she wears the standard skirt
which rides up her legs as she stretches
over a windshield, or bends to a tank.
The boy who led her down basement steps
has gone like a cough in the night.
Gas drips onto her shoe. A man in the car
traces her with his eyes,
she pushes the nozzle in and wants again
the basement smell, the mattress wet as moss,
a warm face burrowing into her neck . . .

By a house where chastity was taught for a century
joyful wind shakes the field of vegetables.
Dresses ashamed of knees and shoulders
long ago turned into rags on hangers.
Ancestors who saw cloven feet on dancers
tap their bald heels in the grave too late.

Heavy with pollen, wind crosses the yard,
climbs the window and laughs
at the grandmother slipping her arm
around the waking child.

NOVEMBER MARE

Our first snow in seven months
rises to the tops of a mare's hooves,
covers harness marks on her neck.

Dirty white, she is piebald with snow.
She stands still until the wind drops
and a red barn returns from the storm.

Down the mountain of her back
she begins to move: one hind hoof
nudges the settled flakes.

Her tail is a spread blonde plume
as she swings that hoof
digging down to a faded weed.

By now she knows the field
has withered from fence to fence
yet she goes on switching

from leg to leg, kicking clear
four circles of dead grass,
brushing the stalks with her lips.

When her head dips low
she hears a thrashing underground—
Summer, a colt buried alive.

AMONG THE ROWS AT 7 P.M.

I bury my hands in rhubarb leaves
and pull supper into a bowl.

"Created from clods"
rises to my tongue, words

rich enough to plant.
Kneeling in half light I touch

tangled roots and weeds,
worms multiplied by a spade,

bones of forgotten horses.
But the oldest fathers

digging the oldest gardens
came from neither clods nor dust,

says the scrawl on the back
of a beetle on my wrist.

A tall red god
shot arrows into ash trees,

and men stepped out of the bark.

SUNBURN AND SLOW MOULTING

Through three days blistered flesh
tightens over all this body,
clawing from within.
I dream of throwing my paddle at the sun.

Black duck among pickerelweed
never brings upon himself
pain like mine
soon to pull off flesh like a shirt.

In this shaded hammock
                    balm
is a single memory:
black duck—who takes a season to molt—
does not skim and drift around
the sun-swamped lake
finding without a moment's search

the cove where I bent over and
saw clouds
            cedars
                    and red face
shift into one upon the water.

Henry Beissel

THE ROCK OF QUINTALA

Quintala is part of the northern coast of the Balearic
Island Formentera, where this poem was written.

The surf plunges its pick blow by ceaseless blow
into the rock, storms drive their rain chisels
into every fissure, hammering wedges between faults,
shattering primeval moulds, to shape and reshape
this ragged cliff. Stone flakes as salt bites
into crevices. The sea is chewing the coast
boulder by boulder. Life has drawn its line here
sharp as a crack. Seagulls weave patterns of flight
winging the blue air on the white shuttle of their cries
across a maze of shelves and ledges
where sometimes a cormorant scans the sea
and impales the horizon with esurient beak.
Their cries tumble down the sheer drop
and bounce back again like silver fish in a waterfall.
On the plateau high above the tide, savin bushes
strum the taut strings of the wind
that have pulled the pines low to the ground.
Green lizards crouch immobile as the russet stones
on which they warm their bellies in a landscape
that must seem lunar to them but for the giant
walking on his hindlegs, and the rosemary shrubs
into which they flit for safety. At night
the Great Bear climbs over the edge of the cliff
and lumbers into the sky. The moon's sickle
cuts down the stars in its path, they fall
and dance like tiny blossoms on the waves
before they sink away like jellyfish. Bats return
to their nests in the Arab tower on the point
that gazes eyeless out to sea where the sun rises
red as a lobster from its steaming mediterranean bath.
Day opens its pale shutters. Not a muscle moves
in the stony face of the cliff. A fisherman

out in his boat stares in the water mirror
where he cast his nets. The gulls are busy
at the loom of light. Abruptly, shock waves
from a roaring jet shatter the delicate equipoise
of voices and silence. Then another engine starts up
yelling clattering a pneumatic chisel hammers
and cuts into the petrified flesh of Quintala.
The earth shudders, the fish dive deeper, the gulls
reel in their tangled net of screams and feathers
swooping at men and machines as if to scare them
off their folly. — Six civilizations failed
to disrupt what one technological generation may destroy.
But the seasons will prevail. The rats are waiting
in cliff holes to gnaw the black ropes of night.
The wind picks up. Slowly the rock of Quintala
drifts through its constellations time out of mind.

Guy Birchard

CREEK AND TREES

the first stream you came up smiling
　　paddling the poem was good work
though the hardest you'd ever done
　　　　　　　(& poor wages)

　　without knowing the country
without even knowing the language
you would undertake to paddle the poem
　　great distances through waters
only the crafty natives ran on instinct

you do/not
　　　　know what you are doing
and the old chief hunkers up the beach
　　knowing and laughing

He likes you and doesn't worry like some old squaw

He figgers you just might make it

STILL LIFE

straight old Chinese brass
　　opium pipe's dragon
　　　　emblazoned weight

rich brass deep sheen
　　burnished bamboo dragon's
　　　　claw maker's mark

tiny upturned bowl
　　finger polished brass
　　　　& bamboo permeable stem

long, tapered, nippled brass
    bit, slim,
        smooth

layers beneath the hard brass
    surface, fierce repeated
        spark in dragon's other

eye

"the hard edges that don't melt"

the hard edges that don't melt
nor the words
            an electric
            saw cutting wood
a dog barking
                    in the distance
loud

            "a choice among the measures"

the body vibrating
        in jarring
                    counter
point or simple

                harmony

a perception of aphids and a rose vine, some
efflorescence on the glass. This

is what's
        before me. I

tremble for the laden earth

Stephen Brockwell

SAILBOAT SONNET

Th' lake wind wispurz a song thru yer sails
Despite yeller mist & refinry breath.
Her eyes reflekt sun shayps on yer brass rayls
Imajes o'blak fish waytin fer death.

But yuh brush yer blond sayl bak in th wind
& edge yer keel nearer t' her algee coat
Yuh bend yer cleen shaven hull az tho blind
T' th' tin cans & garbage that toss in th' float.

I understand. Yur keel lies deep within her,
Yuh sens a union & a det fer all them years
She kept yuh afloat with her cool fingers
Yuh wanna say yull rub away her tears.

Then feel th rhythmic pantin o her waves:
Glide thru & see how supple she behaves.

RAMBLINS

i wuz walkin' with fists in ript pokets
my jaket too she wuz gettin' worn
But i wuz under th sky t' muse wuz born
and my dreams o' love were like rokets

My only pants had a massive hole.
Tom-Thum/dreamer plantin rimes along th way
undr th dippurs ruf all nite id stay
& the stars like bels began t' toll.

& i'd listn sittin at th side o' th road
on thoz cool septembr nites & taste th dew
drippin frum my forhead like 50 er Blue

Yeah! i'd sit in th dark & sing an ode
Yeah! strummin the elastiks o' my shoos
The shoos near my hart so unsolled.

-loosely translated from
"Ma Bohème" by Arthur Rimbaud

ODD MOUSE TESTS

Gall dang !
Th flowrs 're blumin'
Like white mice,
'Ceptin' no one 'll
Shave th fuzz off them Petuls
Ner stik 'em in a maze
And make 'em luk fer food.

Leonard Cohen

I KNELT BESIDE A STREAM

I knelt beside a stream which was manifesting on a polished wooden floor in an apartment above Central Park. A feathered shield was fastened to my left forearm. A feathered helmet was lowered on my head. I was invested with a duty to protect the orphan and the widow. This made me feel so good I climbed on Alexandra's double bed and wept in a general way for the fate of men. Then I followed her into the bathroom. She appeared to turn gold. She stood before me as huge as the guardian of a harbour. How had I ever thought of mastering her? With a hand of chrome and an immense Gauloise cigarette she suggested that I give up and worship her, which I did for ten years. Thus began the obscene silence of my career as a lady's man.

I KNELT BESIDE A STREAM

This curious paragraph is obviously distilled from a longer undated journal entry probably written during the spring or summer of 1975. I give it in its entirety.

Thinking of some times with Alexandra, one night when I wept for the injustice in the world, the promises I made to the weak and fatherless on her double bed. I knelt down beside a stream and I was invested with the high duty to protect them. Someone hooked a feathered shield on my forearm, and lowered a feathered helmet on my head. My left arm armoured, my right arm armoured, the mind fortified. This was not a dream. The stream flowed by me, manifested in a room above the pavement in New York. Later, just before I mastered her, she turned golden in the bathroom, gold and towering, suggesting strongly with an immense chrome hand that I give up and worship her. I think I did. My thighs were so thin she was alarmed. She thought I was starving.

Now I lie in a pool of fat, ashamed before the daisies to be what I am. Eight years ago, and then the obscene silence of my career, while the butchers climbed on the throne, and they hacked the veil away, and they stood there above us grinning, not even bothering to cover themselves. I made a treaty with those who saw, but I broke it under torture. I was divided into three parts. One part was given to a wife, one part was given to money, one part was given to the daisies. And Alexandra herself bound to the world, babies, a cigarette holder, an accent accelerating toward a wordless gargle and swoon in the Poet's Corner. The last time we met, in the lobby of the Algonquin Hotel, I punished her by whispering, "Some of us still take acid."

Distant battles you may say, but God, how ugly your clothes are. You wear them like the ludicrous stripes of bondage. And you are the winners. You are the guards. And even the butchers above you are not in command. I broke under the sentence of loneliness and the wound of my beautiful twin. These veterans are to be avoided, the old campaigns, the view from the foxhole. You can see them tapping away in every garden. And many other spirits complaining, the ground with a voice, the buried fig tree, and now at noon, the sun over the windmill, the signal of the yellow daisies.

THE ABSENCE OF MONICA

She's gone away
   on the morning boat
My heart
   was too young for her
Wind comes over
   the baker's house
sweet with branch
   of burning fir
She'll never comb
   her hair in front of me
I'll never see
   her sweater on a chair
Cinders from the
   chimney float
on the absence
   of Monica
I spent the morning
   with her ghost
We touched the nettles
   painlessly
I carry the bread
   on a piece of string
and now I'm free
   to come and go

THE ABSENCE OF MONICA

From the Notebooks:

Oh the breeze from the baker's oven makes me reel and invent a room
with Monica, windows and her sweater over a chair, her rich family and
her modesty. I never wanted anything but Monica, to be in a room with
her in Europe and to be head of the government-in-exile.
... Excavate the fig tree, elect the municipal council, be kind to the ones
in your kitchen, fill up the years without Monica ...

She is stretched out on the hill. She came back to me from the middle of the water. She is sailing to Piraeus with a young banker. It is an aspect of her generosity to be in two places at once. Who else is coming to the island? There are only two of you. You and your date in the realms of suffering. How dare you climb on Monica to speak theology? That is why you cannot have the room with her in Rue des Ecoles . . .

. . . I buried Monica in this hill, right before my eyes. Some youths violated the site yesterday. They came over the wall when I was inside the house. They got away with a bunch of poppies, actually two poppies, some daisies and a tangle of wild spinach. But they left their ugly footprints here and there. Traces of the unclean boots which have soiled my finest passages . . .

FORMAL IN HIS THOUGHT OF HER

I am certain he will never have her, this man
who sits before the window with his pen and ink,
who has been listening ever since the night began
to the crickets and his clock going in and out of sync.

Look how he is formal in his thought of her.
She makes her way through darkened embassies.
His stunning polaroids demagnetize and blur—
That could be anyone between her knees.

She does not overwhelm him with her absence.
She does not keep him raw as she did once.
He's raised a customs house at every entrance
to search and tax her beauty if she comes.

He is as tired of his longing as her absence
and so are we. Let's go get a drink
and leave him to his altars and his incense
and his crickets and his clocks going in and out of sync.

FORMAL IN HIS THOUGHT OF HER

Roshi poured me a glass of Courvoisier. We were in the cabin on Mt. Baldy, summer of 1977. We were listening to the crickets.
—Kone, Roshi said, you should write cricket poem.
—I've already written a cricket poem. It was in this cabin two years ago.
—Oh.
Roshi fried some sliced pork in sunflower oil and boiled a three minute noodle soup. We finished one bottle of Courvoisier and opened another.
—Yah, Kone, you should write cricket poem.
—That is a very Japanese idea, Roshi.
—So.
We listened to the crickets a while longer. Then we closed the light so we could open the door and get the breeze without the flies coming in.
—Yah. Cricket.
—Roshi, give me your idea of a cricket poem.
—Ha ha. Okay:

—   *dark night (said Roshi)*
          cricket sound break out
          cricket girl friend listening

—That's pretty good, Roshi.

—   *dark night (Roshi began again)*
          walking on the path
          suddenly break out cricket sound
          where is my lover?

—I don't like that one.

—   *cricket! cricket! (Roshi cried)*
          you are my lover
          now I am walking path by alone
          but I am not lonely with you

—I'm afraid not. Roshi. The first one was good.
Then the crickets stopped for a while and Roshi poured the Courvoisier into our glasses. It was a peaceful night.

—Yah, Kone, said Roshi very softly. You should write more sad.

SLOWLY I MARRIED HER

Slowly I married her
Slowly and bitterly married her love
married her body
    in boredom and joy
Slowly I came to her
Slow and resentfully came to her bed
Came to her table
in hunger and habit
    came to be fed
Slowly I married her
sanctioned by none
with nobody's blessings
in nobody's name
    amid general warnings
    amid general scorn
Came to her fragrance
    my nostrils wide
Came to her greed
    with seed for a child
Years in the coming
and years in retreat
    Slowly I married her
Slowly I kneeled
And now we are wounded
    so deep and so well
that no one can hurt us
except Death itself
    And all through Death's dream
I move with her lips
The dream is a night
    but eternal the kiss
And slowly I come to her
    slowly we shed
the clothes of our doubting
    and slowly we wed

SLOWLY I MARRIED HER

It's a long way home down Fairfax to the Santa Monica Freeway, a sinister stretch of the Imagination. The twine of her fragrance sparks above me like an old streetcar cable. Dust of L.A. exhausted springtime in the lever of my headlights, lifting her shade from smoke to smoke among the luminous lane markers. And what is this song but a little night Muzak for those who get out too much, who talk to their divorced wives disembodied between the windshield and the following stars in voices of secret intimacy such as they never used in the everlasting regime of parting

MY LIFE IN ART

This is the end of my life in art. At last I have found the woman I was looking for. It is summer. It is the summer I waited for. We are living in a suite on the fifth floor of the Château Marmont in Hollywood. She is as beautiful as Lili Marlene. She is as beautiful as Lady Hamilton. I have not been denied the full measure of beauty. Nights and mornings we kiss each other. The feathery palms rise through the smog. The curtains stir. The traffic moves on Sunset over painted arrows, words and lines. It is best not even to whisper about this perfection. This is the end of my life in art. I am drinking a Red Needle, a drink I invented in Needles, California, tequila and cranberry, lemon and ice. The full measure. I have not been denied the full measure. It happened as I approached my forty-first birthday. Beauty and Love were granted me in the form of a woman. She wears silver bracelets, one on each wrist. I am happy with my luck. Even if she goes away I will say to myself, I have not been denied the full measure of beauty. I said that to myself in Holston, Arizona, in a bar across the street from our motel, when I thought she would be leaving the next morning. This is drunken talk. This is Red Needles talking. It is too smooth. I am frightened. I don't know why. Yesterday I was so frightened that I could hardly hand a Red Needle to a monk on Mt. Baldy. I'm frightened and tired. I am an old man with a silver ornament. These stiff movements should not be accompanied by tiny silver bells. She must be plotting against me in my bed. She wants me to be Carlo Ponti. The black maid is stealing my credit cards. I should go sailing alone through the pine trees. I should get a grip on myself. O god her skin is soft and brown. I would sell my family graves. I am old enough for that. I am old enough to be ruined. I better have another drink. If I could write a song for her I could pay for this suite. She saw the men in Afghanistan, she saw the riders, how can she stay here with me? It is true I am a hero of the Sahara but she did not see me under sand and fire, mastering the sphincters of my cowardice. And she could not know how beautiful these words are. Nobody could. She could not perceive the poignant immortality of my life in art. Nobody can. My vision of the traffic on Sunset Boulevard through the concrete lilies of the balcony railing. The table, the climate, the perfect physique for a forty-year-old artist, famous, happy, frightened. Six in the morning. Six-o-five. The minutes go by. Six-ten. Women. Women and children. The light gone from Los Angeles they say, the original movie light, but this view of Sunset Boulevard satisfactory in every way. My life in art closing down. Monica sleeping. All the wandering mind is hers. My devotions begin to embarrass me. She should grow tired of them too. I am tired of them now. She is pregnant. Our love-making is sweet because of this. She will not have the child. Six-twenty. We drink Red Needles every night. She tells me of the gay San Francisco world. The weight of her beauty has become intolerable. People in the liquor store actually pop-eyed and double-took as she went by with her long hair and her sacrificial child, her secondhand clothes and her ordinary face mocking all the preparations for allurement here in the heart of Hollywood, so ripe she is in the forces of beauty and music as to frighten me, who has witnessed the end of his life in art. Six-forty. I want to go back to bed and get inside her. That's the only time there's anything approaching peace. And when she sits on my face. When she lowers herself onto my mouth. This feels like doom. This is a pyramid on my chest. I want to change blood with her. I want her slavery. I want her promise. I want her death. I want the thrown acid to disencumber me. I want to stop staring. Six-fifty. Ruined in Los Angeles. I should start smoking again. I'm going to start smoking again. I want to die in her arms and leave her. You need to smoke a pack a day to be that kind of man. When we were on the road I was always ready to drive her to the nearest airport and say goodbye but now I want her to die without me. I started my exercises again today. I need some muscle now. I need a man in the mirror to whisper courage when I shave and to tell me once again about the noble ones who conquered all of this.

THE END OF MY LIFE IN ART

I saw Roshi early this morning. His room was warm and fragrant. Soon he was hanging from a branch by his teeth. That made me laugh. But I didn't want to laugh. Then he was playing my guitar. From above he looked old and tired. From below he looked fresh and strong. Destroy particular self and absolute appears. He spoke to me gently. I waited for the rebuke. It didn't come. I waited because there is a rebuke in every other voice but his. He rang his bell. I bowed and left.

I visited him again after several disagreeable hours in the mirror. He hung from the branch again. He looked down fearfully. He was afraid of falling. He was afraid of dying. He was depending on the branch and on his teeth. This is the particular self. This is the particular trance. He played my guitar. He copied my own fingering. He invented someone to interrupt him. He demonstrated the particular trance being broken by the question: What is the source of this world? He asked me to answer. His voice was calm and serious. I was so hungry for his seriousness after the moronic frivolity and despair of hours in the mirror. I could not answer. Difficult, he said, reaching for his bell. I bowed and left.

Antonio D'Alfonso

TAXIDERMY
to Harry Hill

Madness, indeed;
It is insanity
Being here
Stuffing
This puppet cygnet
With the feathers
Of a silent swan.

SOMEONE IS PLAYING

Someone is playing
hide-and-seek

Peel and Ste-Catherine's
an ugly place to be
they look at one another
in such a hateful manner

a man walks
speaking to himself
he probably thinks
    himself alone
wait until he discovers
the camera that is following him
                    everywhere

Frances Davis

WOMAN

I am wearing the heat and the still air:
I am wearing the invisible disguises that the trees have taught me,
The green sniggerings, poisonous as early apples,
Beauty that stifles and hammers at the eye.
I have studied the deception of exhausted rivers,
The smell of eels broken by freighters,
Afternoons of rich and rotting vegetation,
The violence of the clamshell and the indignant gull.
I have turned to blood at sunset:
I am wearing the seven veils of forests burning;
Tongues of lightning lick at the wounded sky.
Here is my voice raised in lunatic laughter
To the moon that has touched the stone with cunning
In the night that is in me and of me and without surprise.

Only the child who falls out of bed, still dreaming,
Baffles me with his sweat, his cry of recognition,
As if he had seen a face that I have long forgotten,
Human or absolute, beyond these angry vegetable lies.

RESURRECTIONS

Fallen away from me the quilted cloth
the years of earth-walk that a woman wears
the eager watching of another's hungry mouth
the cross-stitch made of other people's stares,
I rise above the needing and the need
to wear myself within one man's embrace;
I am no longer flower or grass or seed
but copper greened and lovely as old lace.
Beyond the ceilinged fibrefill of clouds

some icy freedom lights upon my flesh,
nerves, bones and logic, wings that sing aloud
the stitchless everywhere, till burnt and blessed,
I dive again for love, past earth to sea,
choosing my own deep sensuality.

Jane Dick

MY BREASTS WANT YOU

my breasts want you
so intensely
they lift my body skyward
nipples burning like suns

clamouring for your fiery tongue
storms flood my veins
my skin howls
my breasts carry me
to the heart of desire

i am hollow and full
i cannot hold you more tightly
than this

THE FIRST WHIFF OF SMOKE

i lay there
after you'd gone
just as you'd left me
vulnerable
yet you spoke to me
as you stood in the doorway
as though—
as though i was fully clothed
and sitting across the table.
You know,
you said,
I can smell burning in the hall.
and i knew we would all be consumed.

Louis Dudek

AUTUMN

All day the leaves have been falling.
I thought of snow,
but the ground is covered with yellow meal
        that you can put your foot through
as you go walking, in an eternal still.

Soft as air the dry leaves,
and the dried weed at my doorstep
        a thorny bone as beautiful
as the shape of anything, when seen alone.

'It is all quite dead and finished,'
    you say, as you walk between houses and trees
holding your breath in mild wonder
        at seeing the ghost you will become.

THE PENCIL-CATCHER MISSES

The cat leaps at the pencil
as the poem falls onto the page—
        so I catch at
branches in cold starlight,
mutely attending words, their form
perfect, as the body is,
    beautiful in all its parts.

THE SECRET

Every poet at the beginning
has a lot to learn
         of what is all his own

a uniqueness gradually revealed

never too much, never exposed—
the secret hinted at, left to discover.

Methods as new mazes, leading all astray

until his circumventions and contemplations bring us
to that quiet stage

where he, the chalk-faced immortal
            stands mute and alone.

A TORN RECORD

Nothing that man makes, or believes, is permanent.
I have seen the ruins of cathedrals—
it is only a question of how long
     what is left of them can stand.
A thousand, two thousand years later, they lie forgotten.

Nothing matters forever, what matters now
is desire, at the center of the whirlwind
     where our two pleasures are folded in one rose.
What matters always is energy, how you can laugh,
     your mouth wide and wonderful against the wind.

FRAGMENT OF CONTINUUM

Something in which a fundamental common
character is discernible amid a series of
insensible or indefinite variations.

Soaked in the emotion of autumn
           a wind like a lost dog
squalls through the backyard
           shaking the garbage cover . . .

Black minatory branches
stare through yellow trees

The garden has collapsed
           like a fallen clothesline
on tenting sticks—
           even the flags of weed

turn away from the disgrace of summer
like beggars from an abandoned feast

Stick to your last
           James P. Johnson
jazz composer, wanted to write symphonies
                      but couldn't get them performed

Eubie Blake wanted to write waltzes
                      like Victor Herbert's

Scott Joplin wanted to compose operas
                      (his opera did not succeed)

Stick to your last   As for fame
the less talent the greater the infirmity

A woman weeping in the subway
                      (unwritten poem)

Men in a terrible hurry
           to know the ultimate things—
as against humanistic housekeeping

And the people's history
an accumulation of resentments

If you accept people for what they are you may discover
they're better than you thought they are

Even those monsters of the Terror
                    Robespierre and Saint-Just
'. . . convinced that man is good by nature'

It's to be considered
whether the world might not have been a happier place
if the nineteenth century had never discovered nationalism
            and the revolutionary class struggle
                    and the rights of women

Those new occasions
to bring out the noble savage

Our basic nature (says Pratt)
                    to club one another

$75-90 billion annually
            for wars and weapons

And those 'great Jews' Marx Freud Einstein

they fucked up the western world
                    (Thank you)
Better the good Jews on Main street
than these over-achievers

Sartre describes the self as 'a hole
            in the midst of Being'
                    A black hole

The poet as a black hole

It is neither feeling, nor thought,
                    nor the unconscious process . . .
Arranging the poem

An arrangement
        of poetical pieces
                    (not very poetical)
An order (a kind of poetry)
                    what it is

If it were experience (Mr Leavis)
If plain living were the better poetry
                    why make it of words?

There is always the living

Why make the emotion out of words
                              or an orgasm
Better the real thing

But the poem is not the real thing
                    is not made of the real
It is another thing

'Variations and inflections of the naked self'

Like nature's doughnut machine
                    making the atoms

The key to identity and order

Béla Egyedi

sing cicada

song of the cicadas
        end of the august moon
how long it took to learn
          the cicadas' song

was it always
      all-over
         so sad?
           (i was born old and sad
           and so far away:
             i cannot even remember
             the cicada song
             in my mother's tongue)

ikons of the road

i pick you up
      in tender disgust
           —such a just-soiled kid's uglied underwear
                    after rape—
i pick you up
      you anaemic breakable beauty
            as fragile as a now-fallen virgin crystal
            from the haunted vertical distances:
            a never-deciphered 'message des dieux'
      as delicate as a lily-of-the-valleys
              on a dung-heap
i pick you up
      (pine avenue toward the mountain-stairs)
      bastard beauty of the hurtling howling metal-beasts

                —long long and far gone—
and you left there, alone
                to be battered shaped maimed raped
into a unique beauty
                        ikon of the engines
                                flower of the asphalt:

                        a lace of rust-&-iron

R.G. Everson

GROWING FLAT OUT

In the Muir Woods across the Golden Gate Bridge
in the mountains north of San Francisco
I came on a log that was lying on the ground. One end
of the log was near the bole of an enormous redwood
The other end—thirty feet away—was free
of the redwood shadow. I comprehended slowly
that the log was alive. It was a laurel tree

This laurel had the hard luck to have sprouted
close to the redwood in deep shade. Not withering
the sapling had grown flat along the forest floor
thirty feet or so. Years in shadow!
I imagined the stick no larger around than my finger
feeling among redwood needles and cones for the sun—
straight for the sunpatch. And somehow keeping alive

I could see where the log had turned, free of shadows,
and become the trunk of a California laurel
The bole stood now smooth grey-brown a bit scaly
The leathery leaves and olive-like yellowish fruit
were high above me. I cannot understand
how the log grew flat out across the ground
but now the laurel flourishing beside the redwood
has as good a chance as any laurel in the forest

MAMBA

When the snake—an eight-foot mamba black as Ola the
    poet-farmer
and big around as either of my trembling knees—
showed up inside our screened-porch Eden, I was alone with
    Lawino
Ola's young wife a gentle woman of firm naked breasts
She had fought in the war of liberation
using some of the weaponry hung on the porch and indoor
    walls

We were passing the time of day while waiting for Ola
by drinking his Asha. Lawino had lifted a gourd
to her sunrise lips when the mamba writhed into view nibbling
the stone floor of Ola's porch with a pebbles-embedded snake
    body
dry as central Africa (where we were) in this season

There is a well-known taboo against throwing down water pots
with water in them. I suppose the same taboo applies to Asha
but Lawino the newly-liberated black woman
dropped her gourd and twitched a rifle
    from the porch wall above her

Lawino shot the enormous snake through the head
The mamba dived promptly into Ola's cistern inside the porch.
    Lawino
vanished into the house leaving me entirely alone
with the snake which was down in the cistern beside me

    Ola's young wife the gentle Lawino
with firm naked breasts reappeared carrying a flame-thrower
from the war of liberation. She fired into the cistern
and all eight feet of the mamba looking like a dirty stove-pipe
leaped straight up from Ola's cistern
The snake was hissing like a Montreal apt radiator in February

The landrover appeared from the jungle and Ola
climbed down. He stood in the shamba. He saw the burned
    dead snake
limply gyrating. He saw his wife Lawino seated on the floor of the
wrecked porch, her hands lolling, her head wilted

L'ORIGNAL

The bull moose only a startling rod or so away from me
looked to be about nine feet long
maybe six feet above the trampled down snow
and he would go about a thousand pounds
even though starved gaunt. He was murder-angry had eaten
all the undergrowth and above him all twigs and branches
within reach so that the little forest on his island was trimmed
evenly along the lower parts of the trees
according to the undulations of the land

This mini-skirts appearance of the island had drawn my
    curiosity
as I crossed the lake on the way home with the new axe—
to encounter the terrifying sight at close range of *l'orignal*
as the French long ago named the bull moose having never
seen so strange an animal in Europe (The Indians called him
    mongswa
from which the English took the name the twig eater)

The moose had probably been chased to this island
in the deep of winter. Nearby me on the lake ice lay a long-
    dead wolf
(on a guess, a wolf—I hadn't seen one outside a museum or
    zoo)
frozen at full stretch and partly drifted over.
I figured that the moose had used the small island as a fort
Even after the wolves gave up and went away
the moose may have stayed browsing but the island had
    trapped him

The ice shore had become too weak for a getaway
The late winter sun heating shore rocks
had circled the island with a thin-crusted moat. I observed
where the starving moose had several times broken through
in trying to escape after he had eaten everything within reach
Dimly seeing me out here among pressure ridges
and water pools in the sugar snow over yard-deep ice
the moose probably took me for one of those wolves
so he charged

Immediately he splintered through the ice and disappeared
When he came up on a tide of icicles and water
he kept on trying to get at me slamming
the breaking ice with his forelegs. He had no horns.
I however was having a close look at his front hooves
until he turned around and feebly swam through ice-floes
He was a long time dragging himself up over the shore rocks.

I walked half-way around his little island
and bellied over the thin ice pushing
my axe ahead of me. I didn't quite break through
and ashore quickly inexpertly cut down a poplar
pushing it inland as the moose staggered toward me
The falling treetop confronted his weak charge. The monster
began to nibble on the delicate twigs
In March all deer are starving and weak but this one
was the prize woebegone. His bell was thin as a string
He stayed at the end of the tree and kept eating
while I managed to hack down another poplar and another
ruining our environment and probably breaking some laws
but there was peace between that moose and me. I worked
until I figured that he had fodder enough for break-up
when he could get off the island and swim to a mainland
forest for a fresh start. Then I crawled full length
over the weak shore ice and walked along the lake
in the last of the late-winter day

Patricia Renée Ewing

THE BEAUTIFUL BUTCHER

    god a beautiful butcher carving out his meaty
universe hacking the bright chunks of beef into
continents & kingdoms hammering & pounding the
muscle with the edge of a steel blade parcelling
out his portions slicing territorial rights
god's mouth splits wide in a smile his teeth flash
out white lambs the burnt amber of his flesh contrasts
to the brilliant meat a beautiful moor he stands
huge in his butcher shop his hands gigantic grips
thrusting into the fibres enormous thighs hang from
ceilings legs an eternity long buttocks & bellies
& breasts lie prostrate on the slab-standing in an
inch of sawdust the slab a winking mirror god peers
upon the surface & contemplates his image.

UNTITLED

I have voyaged
in my silver canoe
to the red sands
and the distant sea

Holding my eyeball
before me: a bulwark
against the tide.

Endre Farkas

LETTER TO BILL & NAOMI

I carry the slice of b.c. cedar you sent me
in my pocket
                        and whiff it
on crisp quebec days

I type poems & thank yous
on *made in quebec* paper
                        and on mad days
wonder
will it spit them back in my face
because of 'wrong language'
                        (as if that were possible
                        BULL'S PIZZLE! TWICE! DEUX FOIS)

This will be folded/sealed
stamped/sorted and sent flying
over five provinces that were
                        until four years ago
just colours & answers on quizzes

over ontario
            where I convoluted
    for three days

picked up hikers & wild flowers from the roadside
saw wawa, enough evergreen for years, the sudbury moonscape
and bathed in one of the great lakes

over the prairies
where the sky can and did change its temper three times in one day

Drove with my toes

Awoke one morning to a surrealscape of white horses sleeping astand
Sniffed prairie silence

Realised quickly that I could never fall in love with silos
and was stopped by a real RCMP
who asked if we had open drinks in the truck on-account-of it being Sunday
and he was polite and we said no and he laughed and we laughed

all the way to the rockies—the real thing *hostie*
                    (it wasn't even as scary as the alps
                    or as risky as the look-out on mount royal

and over to Thormanby
where notes from the world wash ashore

where you've built a boat to sail the world around in
where you've got a baby in the belly beginning

from where you send me b.c. cedar to get high on
where this should be by now/
                    last lines reading

the poem between us is the thread
keeps this crazy quilt together

                    love endre

LYRIC

for Leo

It's the kind of six o'clock morning
in the sun-up mountains
                    that step sure
on the gravel road

We stare at each other
on such Huck Finn mornings
and keep as silent as the dew

You want to keep friends as now
;bound by morning suns
                    one for each of us
rippling from shore   to middle   to one

It's the kind of six o'clock morning
in the sun-up mountains
                    that fish don't bite
and we don't mind because
we have stepped into what flows

and it is enough to be caught by that

THE SCRIBE

in the morning
feeds the rabbits/ducks & chickens
keeps order among the piggish pregnant sows
saves the horse from horse-flies
has his breakfast
and goes to his studio

where he swats flies
counts swallows on the 3 wires outside his window

rolls a cigarette in secret
feels guilty

with each puff
schemes a world that is perfect
immediately gives it its independence

thinks in english of how to save the french
thinks about leaving
pauses

scratches his head & crotch
notes how the clouds are Bealy
feels subtle
            gets self conscious
edits a manuscript from b.c.

goes to the can
reads the quote on the wall
                    . . . a place of wisdom, where you clear
            the way/for drink & victuals of the coming day . . .
                                brecht
has 3 tomato sandwiches on whole wheat
& a 50
& reads Hedjia by Anaïs Nin

it is now afternoon
notates the swallows on the 3 wires   like a musical score
listens to the cluck of chickens with one ear
to the music of poetry with the other

stereo

dreams of being not lonely

she   makes it quad

kills a fly
remembers Blake
is not sorry
plans ahead
counts his money
$15.00 & a mini-loto

                money is a kind of poetry
                        wallace stevens
                        v-p Hartford Assurance

insulates his studio
knows the rain will & the cold will come in anyway
fool

inserts a new sheet into the typewriter
misspells typewriter
misspells misspells
stops

went raspberry picking
got pricked & bored
                but thought
better these than words
kept picking/getting pricked/munched
kept an ear open for the poem
straightened my back
saw a hawk

notice the change in tense
notice the change in person

feel tired
        a poet's day is never done
        no rest for the wicked

napped

woke

intrigued by these two ordinary/everyday/unusual words
looks them up
                middle english
both
stops

feeds the animals
begins to care about each sow's individuality
& notes the definite hierarchy

sups & watches french tv
                              (synched bewitched)
swears in french about yankeenization of canader

takes   an after supper walk down a dirt road
is the fulcrum for the see-saw of the sun & moon

helps with the dishes
has two helpings of raspberry pie
                              my/my
how things do come around

food for thought

writes a letter to an american born poet living in canada
I never said he was consistent

peels an orange-orange moon
counts fire-fly lights
pisses under the stars
understand??
ends the epic

makes the night lyric

Raymond Filip

HANK WILLIAMS MEETS THE MUSIC OF THE SPHERES
In memory of Bobby Martin

Still in your teens,
a French-Canadian country slicker,
mouth caught open like a town crier,
executing a number with head cocked shy
of the mike like some amateur night shotgun:
a picture of health and happiness—
that snapshot you showed us before you died,
a brighter shade of the breathing hoodoo
ghosting five-and-dime paparazzi
we blew up for publicity and serious laughs,
a tight trio bottlenecked in one booth,
playing upon stages that were even smaller,
pockets inside out.

Painter, plasterer, freight-handler, garbage picker,
picking up English from crates of comic books,
guitar-picking from skippy Gene Autry 78's,
the Big Time, God's Country, lying in wait,
you hoped—
but only blood pressure climbed,
while your name circulated with street singers
and walkers and hawkers and rip joint owners
where your face found a footing 'til your fingers
and your joints and your throat and your thoughts
all ached for a break—

But only your voice broke,
coming as cheap and wooden as
the ten-dollar Peerless you chorded
like a leper as stardom blurred
into another type of manual labor—
music as monotonous as engine rough,
muggy nights of bandstand steam baths,
riotous cheer no prison riot could rival,
roadhouses rocking and cooking and looking

like boatfuls of buffalos fucking high and dry;
not one eye listening to solos you knocked
off with pills from our amplified outpost,
captured by paying customers smoking pipelines
and joking and soaking and roping their arms
in singing and swaying at beer-banging tables,
opposite removes in rhythm and timing
from our timing and rhythm:
"an audience with the pope."

How many I wonder saw the cancer
you sprayed into dead microphones?
The jaundice yellowing your skin
and eyes as if smeared with cowpies?
The quarrels in dirty dressing rooms
that peed on one more pig of a gig?
You weeping in the woods?
I see your corpse at a kitchen table
slumped forward in a funny final bow,
face buried away in embroidered stars
and monogrammed lamé of old stage clothes
you were mending, the stitching near gone,
all stations signed off, and the TV still on.

NEVER MARRY AN ARTIST

Never marry an artist,
Unless you like starving,
Or eating after immorality.
They're softer than peanut butter melting in the sun,
And just as rich, and smooth, and nutty.

Never marry an artist.
Uncivil and disobedient,
Civil servants can't make heads or tails of them.
They're a curiosity, a brown bag.

Never marry an artist.
There's no money in it.
They're losers.
Marry a critic, or a culture vulture:
The winners, the failed artists.

Never marry an artist.
They're ineligible bachelors,
In knots before you even tie one.
You won't be a golf widow,
You'll be a frisbee widow.
Life will part you worse than death.

Never marry an artist.
They'll divorce themselves from reality
On the grounds of mental cruelty.
They'll carry you over the threshold
Of a new consciousness.

Never marry an artist.
Niagara Falls will roar against it.
They'll want every street they have laughed
And danced and sang on to bear their name,
But be lucky to wind up a number
In some nameless asylum.

Never marry an artist.
Unless you can grow as their gift of communication
Grows in community with you.

Marry an artist,
If you can say:
I don't.

HOUSE PLANTS
(IMPRESSIONS FROM A POISON FLOWER CHILD)
For Liz

The warmth of human touch
Is not always good for them,
These families of plants
Who inhabit the same air
With families of people.
I finger them as carefully as a house of cards.
Coleus, Cactus, Azaleas, Busy Lizzies,
Dieffenbachia as acrid as Diefenbaker.
Simply allow the beauty
Inherent in their nature
To meet our own at level best.
Personification is an abstract
Pest that blights true colors.
Yet, because the cuttings
From my own flesh and bone
Fail to take root:
Cut-up, perennial wit,
The way house plants look at things,
I must appear to them as a laughing stock!

From green thumblings in bottled Edens
To Promethian rubber plants,
Each one sets in motion
The transition from house to home;
Becoming themselves botanical stepchildren,
Hybrid changelings,
Shaped and pruned to a future vision
Fostered by their guardians.
Growing pains against the grain?
Pollen envy?
Freudian slips!
For culture,
I feed them Tchaikovsky's "Waltz Of The Flowers."

I have watched them bending so beautifully toward brighter fields,
Tending toward other gardens,
Begging to be broken from their own matter,
Struggling to grow fat on photosynthesis.

They make me happy.
But if it was theirs to do over again,
They would blossom into birds
And shoot for the light of day
With a new lease on life,
Never to lean again.

Two feet planted firmly and squarely on the ground,
I can germinate my own image,
Or balance, or illumination;
Unlike this disorderly totter of osmotic tangles
Looping into leafy lovelocks
As binding as apron strings.
Picked, peaked, piqued,
They must hate me standing the way I do,
Looking so green yet feeling so gray:
Budding young poet,
Late bloomer,
Cut out to be a man.
Man of the house.

WOODNOTES ON TIMBER

On needles and pine pins,
Decide:Deciduous,
Boreal, real.
Beaver peevers.
Douglas Fee-Fi-Fo-Fum fir trees.
Count them, eat them, wear them,
Run through them,
Until blisters form on your feet as big as resin blisters,
And your heart is the heart of a bird that carries the seeds
Of a branch it has left.
All along the Cabot trail,
In Cape Breton, my eyes stung from the greenness:
Hillsides and hillsides of trees greening the sky.
Even in sleep I saw green.

Or on the Yellowhead,
The whole forest a fantastic forbidding
Stump fence between you
And unneighborly bears.
Trees, stands of time,
Diseased, rampiked, locked like antlers.
Dry rot in the hand,
Driftwood in the rain.
Knotholes the size of wooden nickels.
Goya faces in catfaced bark.

Trees, run through the mill,
Into moonfingers on sunburst guitars,
Crutches at St. Joseph's Oratory,
This poetree!
Trees, Christmas,
"3ft. compact vinyl Canadian Pine with no-shed silver needles"
:Splinter groups.
Trees, that are dwarf trees,
But bear fruit you need a mouth like a giant to bite.

Trees, that fall in the night,
Arms that have lost their balance,
Branches that have lost their leaves,
The better to see:
Stars.

Marco Fraticelli

THE PRISON

here
the seasons have anchors
and drag
windless across dry land

*

STILL LIFE

the newly widowed woman
next door
watering her lawn
in the rain

*

wet blouse
on the bushel of apples
by your bedroom door

*

sparks from your nightgown
the autumn frost on the window
last fireflies

*

spring sunday morning
everywhere the scent of you—
i change the sheets

*

Bill Furey

BURIAL RITES

Bury the dove in the air,
Preferably during starlight,
Do not lay him down
In lake or ground.

Even if the ground is pure,
If his grave is here,
Worms will grow through his heart.
They will hook through his blood
Like that ancient snake of Eden affair,
And tear away his wings for food,
So bury the dove in the air.

Bury the dove in the air.
Insist on lowering him
In the bright sky,
Or instead lay him down to rest in fire,
Or give his small white body
To the voyaging mist—
Carpenter his casket
From the colors of a funeral morning,
Flower it with the reds and yellows
Of a perishing sun,
And stain it with the dust
Of the blue evening stars.

Let the soft breeze carry the coffin.
Weave his shroud from the shreds of mist,
And lower him among the stars
In the high clear sky.
Let the moon serve as light,
And the wind say a prayer
To guard his grave from the carrion worm,
So bury the dove in the air.

LAST THOUGHTS TOWARD THE SKY

I know that when the planets packed my bags
they slipped a few sad feelings in.
But I can't go on believing in their promises.
And so I went on down through the stars
lugging my childhood bundle of hopes,
and thinking of the stars as just white flies
following the moon on its endless pilgrimage;
and with the sun in my face
in vain I mounted the climbing hill
where years before love had been driven.

I've been looking in the wrong places again
for the perfect woman,
and these memories don't help.
I'm mowed down like the grass.
Now she has left again,
I'll lie here in a heap,
the spiders won't notice.
If only passion would let me escape
I could manage in these rags of silence,
love's true refugee.

So tonight I examine the blue autumn stars
in their assaults and exhibitions,
each in its tiny routine of light.
I know they have little to do
with the conditions of love
as I do not suffer beneath them
as much as I do under you.
I suppose I have as much love for the sky
as I do for anything on earth.
This morning I watched the sun push the day out
through its powerful eye
and sift the cold light through it,
but tonight these stars that light the distance
look like nothing more than bridges
that I must burn before I fall,
and know now that they shine brightest
on those who walk individual.

FISH CLOUDS AND STARS

Tonight I think about the fish
who possess no prayerbooks,
no creeds on ocean altars,
whose bodies are impaired
by no meek genuflections,
their very existence
a simple and perpetual hallelujah,
swimming home tonight in silver packs
on the soft spears of the sea.

And clouds, scarves
thrown back over the summer's shoulder,
exist by turning everything in one direction,
shapes in the lamb-like air
combed back into goats' beards,
or plush figures of rams
with sharp horns and marble bleats.
Baudelaire, too, knew the clouds
have no cause to shrink or die.

It's true the stars have limbs and eyes
when we see them as the women they become;
or like benign heroes in the void
they own a sad and noble light.
You ascend in the center of your life
with hair and pencil,
you paint them black,
you color them gold,
with long and prejudiced shadows.

Gary Geddes

THE ANIMALS

We began as dark eyes
in dark places,
reluctant to keep
appointments.

A shape emerged
from the shadowy poplars,
pumping action of knees
in deep snow, rifle
sloped casually down
across a forearm
and dragging something
behind, something dead
to put in a poem.

No names were given, then,
to what we saw.

So we retreated
further into ourselves,
our disguises, until
we were only words
pitched for oblivion.

Our dust settles
in the spaces behind walls.

SANDRA LEE SCHEUER

(Killed at Kent State University on May 4, 1970
by the Ohio National Guard)

You might have met her on a Saturday night
cutting precise circles, clockwise, at the Moon-Glo
Roller Rink, or walking with quick step

between the campus and a green two-storey house,
where the room was always tidy, the bed made,
the books in confraternity on the shelves.

She did not throw stones, major in philosophy
or set fire to buildings, though acquaintances say
she hated war, had heard of Cambodia.

In truth she wore a modicum of make-up, a brassiere,
and could, no doubt, more easily have married a guardsman
than cursed or put a flower in his rifle barrel.

While the armories burned she studied,
bent low over notes, speech therapy books, pages
open at sections on impairment, physiology.

And while they milled and shouted on the commons
she helped a boy named Billy with his lisp, saying
Hiss, billy, like a snake. That's it, SSSSSSSS,

tongue well up and back behind your teeth.
Now buzz, Billy, like a bee. Feel the air
vibrating in my windpipe as I breathe?

As she walked in sunlight through the parking-lot
at noon, feeling the world a passing lovely place,
a young guardsman, who had his sights on her,

was going down on one knee as if he might propose.
His declaration, unmistakable, articulate,
flowered within her, passed through her neck,

severed her trachea, taking her breath away.
Now who will burn the midnight oil for Billy,
ensure the perilous freedom of his speech?

And who will see her skating at the Moon-Glo
Roller Rink, the eight small wooden wheels
making their countless revolutions on the floor?

THE ONLY REAL FORMALISM IS SILENCE

Now they are pure.

They have purged themselves
of all content,
they are cleaner than geometry.

They paint their dreams
upon the water, dispensing
with line and colour

write legends in the sky like clouds.

Critics will declare them
masters.

TECHNIQUE

Is it really, as Pound says,
the test of a man's sincerity,
how he crafts or executes
the perfect poem of our dying?

Were the Nazis more sincere
than the English, or Belgians
eating the dark heart of Congo?

Did the Americans have it over
the Japanese by a long shot,

two long shots?

John Glassco

I AM FAR FROM EASY SITTING ON THIS CHAIR

I am far from easy sitting on this chair
And the clasp of an armchair is the worst of all
There I am bound to drowse and die.

But let me cross the torrent by the rocks
Pass bounding from one thing to another
I find my buoyant balance between the two
It is there in suspension that I am at rest.

—translated from Saint-Denys-Garneau

NOUS NE SOMMES PAS DES COMPTABLES

We are not book-keepers

Anyone can see a dollar is made of green paper
But who can see through it but a child?
Who like him sees wholly freely through it
Without letting the dollar or its meaning stand in the way
Nor its value of just a dollar?

No, he sees through this shop window thousands of wonderful toys
And he has no desire to choose among those treasures
Neither the appetite nor the need
Not he
For his eyes are wide enough to possess them all.

—translated from Saint-Denys-Garneau

PINES AGAINST THE LIGHT

In the light their leafwork is like water
Islands of clear water
On the black of the spruce shadowed against the light

They are all flowing
Each feathery plume, and the spray
An island of bright water at the branch's tip

Each needle a lustre a thread of living water

Each plume a little gushing spring

Running away
Who knows where

They are flowing as I have seen in spring
The willows flowing, the whole tree
Nothing but silver all lustre all a wave
All watery foaming flight
Like the wind made visible
And seeming
A liquid thing
In a magic window.

—translated from Saint-Denys-Garneau

BOUT DU MONDE!

The world's end! The world's end! It's not so far!
We thought in our heart it was an endless journey
But we discover the flatness of the earth
The earth that image of ourself
And now here is the world's end itself
We have to stop
We have arrived

Now we must find out how to make the pilgrimage
And how to return, with backward steps, from where we
      have come

And how to return, against the current, from our illusion
Not turning our head toward the new voices of our riches—
We have already waited too long, pausing all alone
We have already lost too much heart in pausing.

We huddle around the emptiness of what we do not have
The one acceptable reality of what we might have had
Colonies and possessions and a whole belt of islands
Things made in their likeness and sparked here in the absolute centre of what
    we do not have
Which is what we desire.

—translated from Saint-Denys-Garneau

THE GAME

Don't bother me I'm terribly busy

A child is busy building a village
It's a town, a county
And who knows
                By and by the universe.

He is playing

These wooden blocks he is moving around are houses and castles
This board stands for a sloping roof   it looks all right
It's quite a job to know where the cardboard road will turn
It could change the bed of the river altogether
Because of the bridge with its fine reflection in the water of the carpet
It's easy to have a big tree here
And put a mountain underneath to raise it up.

Pleasure of play! Paradise of liberty!
And whatever you do don't set your foot in the room
You never know what might be in that corner there
Or whether you won't be crushing the dearest invisible flower of all

Here is my box of toys
Full of words to make wonderful patterns
To be matched divided married
Now they are evolutions of a dance
And the next moment a bright burst of the laughter
You thought was lost

A light flick of the finger
And the star
That was hanging carelessly
At the end of a flimsy thread of light
Falls in the water and makes circles.

Who can dare doubt his love and tenderness
But not a cent's worth of respect for the established order
Nor for politeness and its precious "discipline"
A levity and deportment to shock grown-up people

He arranges words like silly songs
And in his eyes you can read his mischievous delight
At seeing how he is shifting everything around under the words
And playing with the mountains
As if he owned them.
He turns the room upside down till you don't know where you are
As if it were fun simply to fool people.

And yet in his left eye while his right is laughing
The weight of another world clings to the leaf of a tree
As if this could be of tremendous importance
Could count as much in his scales
As the Ethiopian war
In England's.

—translated from Saint-Denys-Garneau

*When this anthology was begun in 1977, John Glassco was alive and well;
sadly he died before the book was completed. —Eds.*

Artie Gold

Untitled

More things interrupt my work
than carry it on, yet
some things do carry it on. I
open letters, see a note on
the night kitchen counter—
a dear friend of the dear friend
that I live with has died
is to be buried tomorrow
and the phone rings while I am reading
and on the phone is my mother and her
brother, my uncle has died and he also
must be buried. neither of these deaths
affect me but they
affect those closest to me
I am being
buzzed by death. my companions' companions
go down
and they worry about me
and I feel like the body in a hammock
tied both sides onto two trees and no
tree I am tied to
touches me. In the center
 I swing
sideways, while death
moves on
ahead. I feel my marvellous life, untouched
and I skirt both boards on a narrow runway.

OLD ROAD POEM SONG

I have no astrologer—
and don't believe in falling in love
on any particular August day you could name

I have knapsacks full of knick-knacks
that spread beneath a tree
would suffocate a hermit

and a perpetual cough
that when I've had enough of—
I'll die from.

I came to this city
naked   and from a small town
and have rearranged some of its objects

I will hitch-hike out of here one day
with my hair in my eyes and a good breeze blowing
and cause a little confusion I'm sure—

though no more than a hair
discovered in a gravy.

You

leaning, like a Hardy Boy
I touch my fingers lightly
to the invisible panel

if I listen, *fear* falls away
how are you?   over, the green hills
the panel swings, revealing—

revealing summer. daylight
roars from the spot. Above me
you stand like an easel

I lean my face sideways
tenderly towards you, nuzzle.
like an artist who has lost his brush

and what he'd begun to do
bending over, *was simply to retrieve it*
and then, *he fell in love with an idea...*

DON'T STOP CLAPPING TILL I'M FAMOUS . . .

It was the greatest poetry reading Canada ever heard
AJM Smith was there with his polaroid land camera
Earle Birney stood by the door flipping his lucky
                                        both-sides-beaver nickel
The Governor-General smiled like a Parisian-born trick
you could hear everywhere hoofbeats of moose & windblown birch boughs
Everyone was related to everybody else.
Across the audience smiles broke like quebec bridges
I kept thinking the face on the very next guy to read was the
splitting image of an autumn-blown maple leaf atop Mount Royal
we threw the critics out early in the show
they asked the poets the wrong kind of questions and we just knew
they'd leave early and cause trouble for us
                                    /at the *banks*)
famous people read aloud and no smart-asses coughed at crucial points
the concluding speech told you what the next fifty years of canadian
poetry would be like, whereupon
All stood
And the flag
was raised & lowered by the unseen hands
of Robert Service's ghost who'd been with us since intermission.
I was proud
alka-seltzer-proud . . .

a patriot was stationed at each exit and it was the patriot's duty
to after each poet had read/fling open the door to the subzero howling
winds which beat at all our faces and cold that turned the sweat on our
cheeks to icicles/while a sign was held up above the stage's dais which
read:
        DON'T STOP CLAPPING FOR A MINUTE FOLKS
            OR YOU'LL NEVER HOLD ANOTHER PENCIL BETWEEN
                YOUR FROSTBITTEN FINGERS
                                        —thank you,
                                        —merci.

Poem

The rain has stopped
but left everything so sad
wet and sad. I offer my hand

into the sky, past the
roof of the tent my jacket makes
it tastes no dryness yet. The sky

recalls in its strange manner
demands what has fallen
back from the grass. I pass

a wet red fire
hydrant glistening the rain
has made it fantastically rich

and along the concrete ditch
an orange cat rushes
its coat dry.

Looking up the source the sky
is beautiful mysterious
with clouds moving quickly disbanding.

1 april 68. mtl

Raymond Gordy

AFTERNOON VISITOR

She came, answering my call
At the open door standing
I, withering like breath
To her nearness.

We talked, spoke of each other's wants
Arranging them as if on paper
Hiding almost nothing
Holding back only for the tension.

Poetry, you have me
The high voice still carrying
You, skipping across the eyes
Hands gone out!

Wine to our lips
We drank, we drank it all
And in this happiness did not miss
The little that was spilt.

BERRY-PICKERS

Trained, we the five rustle bushes
For berries. Round and blue
From under the leaves they stare
To the sudden turning in our hands.
Plucked, in our bowls they loose
The wind, trees, sun as we bend,
Intent on stripping clean, the colour
From this tranquil wild scene.

Ralph Gustafson

THE EMBER

The fire hisses, the logs,
Cut into fourteen-inch
Lengths, work on the flames,
The wetness scorched out the ends

So that the embers, scarlet
In serried cracked combs,
Steam. The clock hesitates.
Daylight goes and winter holds.

House-nails ungrip
In the boards. Snow creaks
Though there is no step,
Only of that morning.

I put more wood on,
Heat moves air,
Outside, up
From the chimney. Warmth

Is near the hearth, on
The stairway, cold.
Cold enters on the stairs,
On the hearth, flames.

Lengths hiss with wet and the
Sap of far woods,
The path filled, the steps
With snow. The oil

Burner comes on. I pick up
A shot ember in my fingers,
Flesh quick to get rid of it,
Heart tentative.

WEDNESDAY AT NORTH HATLEY

It snows on this place
And a gentleness obtains.
The garden fills with white,
Last summer's hedgerow
Bears a burden and birds
Are scarce. The grosbeak
Fights for seeds, the squirrel
Walks his slender wire.
There is a victory;
The heart endures, the house
Achieves its warmth and where
He needs to, man in woollen
Mitts, in muffler, without
A deathwish, northern, walks.
Except he stop at drifts
He cannot hear this snow,
The wind has fallen, and where
The lake awaits, the road
Is his. Softly the snow
Falls. Chance is against him.
But softly the snow falls.

TUONELA

This stone flung in space.
I'd be north,
north on it.
Mist rings the mountains,
barren,
barren in the valley
the slopes,
cold snows,
streams
falling north
which is the need,
snow on the peaks,
no sound,

place
of rock.
I pick solitary this flower,
this single delight
grown beside moss wet with mist
beside rock
deathward which is
north,
I write this down
deathward.

Jack Hannan

ASSUME A VOID

Assume a void exists without
the hands of your own need, and already
something moves toward filling it,
so even in that silence you can trust
plain song, what felt like nothing, becoming.
The character of that silence moves out into the clear
of the valley, the lights, the silence
is of listening before you go on, as it comes
into your head, a young girl's sleepy eyes closing
at midnight, dreaming
the attraction of things, the mountains, the lovely
textures of the distances she will travel. Someone sings
her, and she dreams my whole world, the song
mustn't end before the dreaming.

THERE IS A PIANO

There is a piano, which is
an old photograph on a hill, soft light, soft focus, full of
suggestions. What would you have said to Trakl anyway?
Icons of his sister and muddy boots, his fondness
for loud minor chords in the lower registers.
Far off the hill a car moves, he says
its round white eyes cork the night, he mumbles something
which you later interpret as "Grete,"
horses in the moonlight are all long legs and necks
bent down to the lake for water,
the moon's reflection at their heads,
as you approach they run off, he says, vanish
with the moonlight,
leaving the crickets to hold down the dark, and all around them
is soft chaos, full of suggestions

"THE WORK GETS COMPLETED IN A DREAM"

We have our intentions, finally
which seem decipherable only at outside moments,
one can be saying one thing while
those listening watch you
act out another, and for a second there
you catch something of yourself
in the look in their eyes

You come upon it in that mirror
and those of what's left, a woman's
pins and elastics by the wash basin, or what I did
with the money that I had, or another,
a set of words aimed at some vague thing
which turns out afterward, whenever
they seem right, always the one
same thing

In the home pieces your name is mentioned
along with the lamp on the table
of what you've given me, and I'm grateful for

Of the various tones of light in the way
the room changes through time, someone
studied you there, now one can see
what was in mind

Tuesday and another Wednesday, this land
is all an echo now, how it slopes down somewhat
where you are, knowing
what you know can only turn
that one way, the slowness the shape uses
to draw itself out, no rush, no other wishes

SHE WAS GOOD TO POOH

He was lumbering and there were two
big brown bears wearing collars and ties and pork
pie hats and their awkward dancing
became quite graceful and he knew
that this was her doing for only she
could cause such a thing, it was a trick she played
by changing the light, he could balance
on his unicycle and his voice
improved with the singing, he lay a mason jar
down on a hill and she filled it.
He has asked me recently if I knew all this
and I replied that by the asking he'd
confirmed my suspicions, and he asked me
if I knew what's come of her since, and I said yes sir
that's my baby now.

Michael Harris

THE GAMEKEEPER

The salmon is still
in the noiseless black; she was quick-silvered
            star to the ship whose hull
      has sunk below the bottom of the lake.
            The weeds stand stiff
in the shivering dark, and the gamekeeper's gone

whose bears are now shadows
long done with their powers
            in the mud-and-cold land.
      The vixen's neat paws print
            the news in black stars
but the secret's gone quick
            and dug deeper. Autumn's hold
      has been broken
a million times over
and it's snowing.

The bright hummingbirds flew
      to find their hearts in
      a frenzy, for the sky was a flower
that had lost its center
            and the swarms in the air
were snow. Now they know all there is to know
of dark. And the gamekeeper's gone

whose crow's a tattoo
at the top of a tree, losing his grip
      at the too-thin top
of the cold that is pricking him bare.
            He thinks war
and it's war though the summer's surrendered
      and raised its white flag
a million times over
and it's snowing.

Now the waddling porcupine's swaying his quills
      all at sea in the swaddle
            of his winter fat;
he is slow in the sudden
      and no match at all
            for the silk and soft skins
of winter. He chews bark,
for the gamekeeper's gone

whose snakes took green with them
      and wove it in a bundle
          and buried it under a rock,
for the earth had stopped in tatters
      and lay down dead-white
          dead-skinned, belly-up
and not right. Then the wind coiled hugely,
      struck and coiled and shed its white
a million times over
and it's snowing.

Plump rats and grey weasels channel blindly
      their fright, clawing squealing
at their tunnels: to core them, seal them, escape
      from the light, from the ache
of a world wide with snow; but their black brains
are caught, are furnaced with the spark:
the gamekeeper's gone

whose starving, still hopeful, pure panic of deer
      tiptoe the brittle-twigged landscape to silence
to a deadhalt
at the appletree; and the appletree's victory stays
      stiff-necked, full of thrash
in its iron-bare head of black antler,
in the slow-moving barrens of its branches
      where the sky falls to pieces
sinking deeper and deeper
a million times over:

and it's snowing on the otter
whose eye is a film of ice.
It whispers blessing the shivering field-mouse
whose heaven is black with snow.

It is snowing on the hare
whose fur is a layer of winter.
It falls against the houses,
against the drinkers in the bars,
a million times over. The gamekeeper's gone.

The fields harden fast
around their stone.

OWLS HOOING AT MY HOUSE

Entirely the size of my thumb, a mouse
came a night ago on pink feet

poking its nose one blind inch, and one
inch more, insistent and dim: an intruder, destroying,

with nibbles and squeaks, my perfect wall, my peace.
Three years to ready the house for this winter:

careful measurings and cuts, the stuffing
in every corner, the wallseams silent and

finally breathless. The thing moved in
and out of the wall, at will.

I set a trap to crack its neck, thinking
if I can't control the cold, the simplest flaw,

I could civilize rage, at least, and kill it well.
Then heard the owls, floating coolly by the house;

and got the mouse to go, then patched the hole.
Then turned my face to my faulted wall, and slept.

THE ICE CASTLE

Even now, mid-winter,
something light, alive,
is shining from the depths of it.

When I touch its perfect skin,
the light shimmers melting
in small streams of water.

How delicate the dream
that even ice
attempts to hold.

THE COVE AT NIGHTFALL

1.

In these imprecisely
heaving tons of iron

the skiff keeps its head
toward the island.

Scaling the marble
sides of the sea, she lifts,
from the opening gutters, her gunnels

and stresses and slides easily down
the last waters to the beach.
High up on the near hill,

plain grass and grey rock;
and a scattering of careful-stepping,
civilized, poker-faced sheep.

2.

Not a candy-wrapper
on the miles of beach;

not a fish not parsley-dotted
neatly in the shops that run

row-on-row in a curve-around
that obstreperous, out-of-hand,

roiling and red-faced, stagger-drunk sea.
How the winds and waters relentlessly conspire

against these folk. They take
from clammy damp good whisky.

They grow their roses
out of sand.

3.

The boat rests like a seagull
in the air, wheeling to find its head,
tired from too much weather.

The slops of water run by the gunnels,
a lulling murmur. The sky is clear, and rich
with stars; and the cove-water blurs

with plankton. Now is the time for simple
histories, and sleep. And dreams of dark waters
deeper than this mooring-rope. Of dark skies

deeper than the mast. We survive; and stir
the idle heavens with our masts; and with
the frailest of our sailings break the sea.

Aran, Scotland

Neil Henden

ADEQUATE DESCRIPTIONS

When she sleeps
               there
                    are
pieces of fruit
               covering her eyes

          when she sleeps
Her hair is tied back
                    like
                         a
                              nylon snake
(Yes ye old catgut slimy toothed viper you)

          while she sleeps
A shirt pulled tight
                         over
                    her
                         petite body
(emptied fast and quickly)

          as she sleeps
Old barns emptied fast and quickly
are like grey sculptures
                         in
                              this
                                   grease ball town
(Yes ye old greaseball, greyhaired town you)

          when she sleeps
Ancient and contemporary
                         jazz
                              styles
                                   play me
(gold in my mouth and in hers)

          while she sleeps

THE WOMAN ON THE FIRE ESCAPE

An old Greek woman
beats rugs with a metal stick
rain shines from her hair

EVEN IN OUR MOST VIOLENT DREAMS

And so we
       raise our moist moon eyes
       like glasses of beer to a mindwell
       of shattered mirrors.

And so we
       bleed small poems
       that bounce on the pavement
       like rubber balls.

And so we
       see Negro faces
       in everything that reflects.

And so we
       see an elderly man,
       an image in a broken sentence.

And so we
       see Christianity
       in a bottle of the Old Cutty Sark.

And so we
       have a warm feeling
       in our bodies.

And so we
       love each other
       even in our most violent dreams.

Laurence Hutchman

TWO ORANGES

Snow hangs on the fence,
the air is cold blue,
death a dark window.

I am learning to feel.
Before me two oranges
in a brown bowl.

I hold them,
feel their weight rise
through my fingers into my arms.

In this silence before sleep
I place two oranges
within the rim of our lives.

GIRL WALKING ON FRIDAY AFTERNOON

Over the sidewalk she moves
her coat dark above her hips.

Nor does she alter that pace
moving under the stained glass
myths, the gothic domes.

Evenly she moves
through melting snow
by running water
up toward mountain boulevard.

She stops, turns
raises three curled fingers
to the strands of her hair
glances into the bright wind
    steps down into the street.

BALCONY

Glancing at my directions
for the number of your house on Ste. Famille
    those Parisian fronts with Brooklyn railings
across Sherbrooke tarnished figures from antiquity
    then you two waving from a balcony.

On the doorglass a pastel flower
blooming:
            bound up the stairs
as they give way, waves
leap up into the light of your apartment
    music of Morocco swirling
through Greek pillars, crystal chandeliers,
    a mosque glimmers in dark water
in an alcove of a photo
                        people are waiting
you on the balcony by a rusty railing
waiting: pigeons, grey, mauve, green feathers
rise through heat
            vertigo
    and so here we sit on this shaky balcony
above Ste. Famille
            and talk
about Indian rhythms, Black rhythms
    and one floor down
a girl in a blue garb
    sits before her round red table
                café, fromage et croissants.

Soon in the yellow kitchen
the lady and the unicorn singing
singing of Mallarmé's angel
    and out there
    in the lavender light skies
the sun setting on the green mountain
    our dark bodies outlined,
the balcony,
        glowing.

D.G. Jones

A GARLAND OF MILNE

He lived in the bush, the wilderness
but he made light of it

He was at home, sitting
with the small birds around him
gathering seeds, the bare

earth showing through the snow
the sun falling
scenting the air

For him it was a garden

Wildflowers picked in the woods
he placed in a pickle jar
perhaps to sketch

A tent made a pleasance

He let the trees stand where they were

and he went quietly
where islands curled up for the winter

A wife could not abide
that god-forsaken country

but a woman came
as silently as trees
and stayed

being cut in the grain, like Eve

He wanted nothing

He lay in wait for ponds, the still
moments when the snow
fell from the branches

Flowers he knew most naked in a bowl

He left it to Monet to paint
the waterlilies in their wild
and dangerous state

The titans he contained in a cartouche

A battlefield or a deserted house
had a life of its own

No violence

Who flies with the whirlwind is at rest

No one in France
could make such galaxies
of glass and water

intricate with flowers

All space came out in flowers
miraculous, erupting from a void or mouth

And every breath
a wind or sun, a season or delight
drew colour from the earth

as if a brush
stroked virgin canvas

The hills flew little flags beyond
the painting place

The darkest night drew fires
like jack-o'-lanterns from the street

The children danced like flames

And gaily, gaily glowed the islands
under the storm's spout

The light was never spent

A solemn gaiety awoke
in the white poppy

amid the sanguine and magenta reds

THE POEMS OF CH. ANYONE

i
OK, OK, I looking fine
I see she swing she walking home
I see the cutlass how she go
through water quick and leave no line

ii
Mistress come like beau bateau
cream and cocoa le matin
fine people leave and walk around
I swim for quarter down below

iii
Blackbird stepping on my roof
make more noise than little stones
head she sound like blackbird when
she think how I become rich man

iv
Small lizard hanging on my door
keep flies away from my new girl
pawpaw spill her seeds in bowl
coconut spill milk on floor

v
Smoke from coal pot fill my house
woman's talk she bite me too
I pay high price for flying-fish
I pay for her big belly too

vi
Child you are no child no more
rooster see you, girl, he crow
keep that basket on your head
take those legs from my front door

LES PETITES POMMES CE SOIR

for Monique

Les petites pommes ce soir
tombent comme les jours

comme les êtres de l'arbre de vie

comme nos désirs

Elles sont petites et rouges et un peu dures

et si nombreuses
éparpillées dans l'herbe, luisantes
dans la lumière et dans la pluie

Les petites pommes font 'toc' ce soir
comme une horloge qui boîte
et dit le temps d'une façon inégale

mais vraie

J'écoute
les petits chocs, ouatés un peu
par l'épaisseur de la nuit

J'écoute
le temps des pommes

Que tu es loin ce soir de ces pommiers

Jim Joyce

DANDELION

The dandelion's real flower
is white, round,
a transitory bloom
for the subtlest of winds.

Yellow its ugly-duckling stage,
a simple dish which expands
into a sphere in order to throw
its tufted arcs.

Yesterday, there was a field
of glass bulbs, and then today
only their green fists,
the white brainstorms carried

to neighbors' lawns, vacant lots.
All life should improve with age,
adult stage beyond bloom,
careless about posterity.

Janet Kask

BLUEBERRIES

It isn't only
that they're beautiful,
blueberries, blue on green,
powder blue over the blue
that shines royal blue when the
fingers dust them.

But when you touch them,
then you touch the lips of babies
and at the same time
the sheen of polished stones.
You get the lightning sparks of
your skin
on my skin.

And when you take them,
when you tear them
from their green crowns,
when the smooth pale and royal blue skin
breaks,
they bleed.

MUSHROOMS

You hunt for mushrooms
like old and fecund thoughts.
Your sharp eye scans the ripe bush floor
for pictures.

On the moss, the photos pass,
slowly as aging.
A red coated girl appears,
carrying a basket.

In Poland the mushrooms also bloomed
beneath the mountains, and women with baskets
gathered with pilgrims,
honouring the shrines.

Another picture,
then another.
A young wife feeds her fowl.
Sunflowers hang in the air.
The voices of small children
rise
and fall
and disappear.

More photos.
You cannot make them out.
But now you see the pits of burning bodies,
the barbed wire meadows of flesh.
You will not gather these.
They stay hidden in the underbrush
of your bewildered eyes,
lethal, red-flecked
Death Angels.

DOMESTICUS

Wanting everything
for you,
tidiness of mind,
bedsheets tucked in
at the corners.
Flowers in every
room for you,
every moment guarded
with needle eyes,
ready for threading.
This love is constant,
often hidden, but
fine in sunlight
as particles
of dust.

Tom Konyves

EIGHTY CENTS CANADIAN

First a flower...then a bee...
then a thistle...

along the waterfront
early morning drizzle of warm rain.

the only moving thing
was the sign of the .10% sign.

I promise not to say fuck
in bad company.

Diogenes said the world is your oyster.
I disagree.

REBEKAH

I saw Rebekah approach the well.
In my ears Isaac had begun the afternoon prayer.

Rebekah,
young, her hair pulled tightly back.

An angel came during the night and slew
her father, Bethuel, in divine fashion.

I was sleepwalking among the camels
and they were terribly nervous.

LEONARD FOUND POEM 1976

Leonard found a quarter in the yard,
embedded in ice.
He said
"Get something"

I did.

ANOTHER CREATION

On The First Day
I forgot to ask about the appearance. I
was busy listening to the slide guitar player
pretend.
And that was good.

On The Second
No use wasting space in the infirmary,
I overheard the matron. I reach down
to ring the bell. No answer.
And that too, was good.
Coming, coming!

On The Third
Walking down The Main.
I'm thinking about the union of Sun and Moon.
Stores close slow,
she's on time.
She was very good.

On The Fourth
I found it.
Hurrah for the old team!
Hurrah for the old town!
Really, it was very good. And everyone
understood.

On The Fifth
What is it? Robinson Crusoe
called a man Friday. Graffiti.
What is it? Only the shadow of my hand on the paper.
Shadow games. Gorilla.
Is your hearing good?

On The Sixth
Nothing but the hobby-horse of God
on the horizon. Creak, it goes.

On The Seventh
In the evening, we used to walk together
in the garden. There was no treasure,
only iceboxes and feverish women in jeans
holding hands. I didn't think to count them.

Rochl Korn

(Translated by Seymour Levitan)

CRAZY LEVI

And no one knows what became of him, Crazy Levi,
who tied the roads
from Yaverev to Moshtsisk
to Samber to Greyding in a bow,
carrying always in his breast pocket
his letters to Rivtshe,
his uncle's youngest daughter.

All the houses in the villages knew him,
the road accepted his long shadow
like a horse that knows its rider,
and the dogs lay quiet in their doghouses
when the familiar smell of Levi's flaring black coat-tails
spoke to their canine hearts.

Women broken in the middle like sheaves
were in the field when Levi came by.
They toyed with him
and with a laugh that smelled of goodness, like dark bread,
they would say,
"Levi, you have no father or mother.
Why don't you take a wife
like the rest of your people?
She would wash your shirt for you
and cook you a spoonful of something warm for supper."

And Levi would look at their raw, swollen feet
and plow the brown field of his forehead
with the painful thought that was always present to him:
"Because my uncle wouldn't give me his daughter for a
wife.
I carry my heart around
like a cat in a sack,
and I want to leave it somewhere
so that it won't be able to find its way back to me."

And he would take a filthy piece of paper
out of his breast pocket
and read aloud from a letter in German,
"An Liebchen!"—
and a red berry would blossom in the dark moss around his lips:
Levi's crazy, melancholy smile.

But after one long hard winter,
worse than any the old people could remember,
the small eyes of the window-panes
looked for Levi without finding him
and the dogs put their heads to the ground
and sniffed at all the tracks on the road,
thinking he might have come by—

And to this day, no one knows what became of him.
maybe the hungry wolves in the woods tore him to pieces
or maybe his mother who hanged herself in her youth
missed her son, and a small, white hand
reached out to him from the dark attic of the old house.

BERL'S COW

He sold the one-horned cow
and let the money blow through his fingers
like pieces of spiderweb.
And ever since then, the stall has been empty
as the hole in a gum after a tooth is pulled,
The chain at the trough is rusty and cold,
and Berl's children haven't seen a spoonful of milk in
the house
all winter

When the woman next door milks her cow,
Berl's children stand around her like chicks
around a mother hen.
Ten pairs of eyes staring eagerly
at the warm white streams.

Berl goes to the market in town every Monday,
pokes the cows, examines their teeth, and bargains.
But it's always someone else who buys the cow
and always Berl who comes home from market
with a can of gasoline, kasha, and a sack of salt.

Helen Kosacky

I MUST STEER IT CAREFULLY

I must steer it carefully;
    i must lead the tiger very carefully, for i control his leash. He will
try to pull me, roll me over—anything to get the throne. Bullrushes guard
this narrow path.
    It is not a path at all;
                it does not figure
                        on any map.
My feet lose their practise; my sneakers fill with mud;
      the sneaker tries to stalk me like a tabby;
          i rattle his leash. He stops in surprise.
Outside the lamps are lit, each defined by its own halo.

We are borrowers, sharing haloes amongst ourselves.
We must treat them carefully, sip them cautiously like a great rare wine.
I ignore the tiger's efforts to upset my glass;
     i do not want
             to be spilled all over the carpet.

THE MUSIC PLAYS AND PLAYS

The music plays & plays
              instrument-less, soundless: all you are
                    is music.
It climbs the walls like grapevines,
       the realization
               of Keats' lofty vineyards.
You drink the coffee, eat the cake,
        your head is not
           your own.
The ceiling expands like a fine balloon, eyes mellow like little
stars, medulla & the angels find
          new dance-steps to creep through.

The world becomes a
                buzzing guitar string
                                ready to feed whole lifetimes.
The tiger in the
        form of musician
                proudly wears the stage:
You realize you've been seeing
                (in)carnations
                        for a long time now.

Greg Lamontagne

THE DRUNKEN BOAT

As I descend down the naked rivers,
I no longer feel myself guided by my haulers' fingers.
Screaming redskins had taken them for bait,
Luring my drunken boat to a sharp stone stake.

I cared not about the crew,
Porters of Flemish wheat and Bastard cotton.
With them gone the uproars were through,
And I could float down the river alone, and forgotten.

In the ripping of foam and fuzz,
My thoughts were as simple as a child's mind.
I ran from the shadows of peninsulas,
Who offered me coral lifelines.

The storm has painted the morning sky red,
And I drift like a cork on the water's tiles.
People roll by cold and dead.
It's been ten nights since I've seen a harbor's smile.

Like the skin of a sour apple to an infant,
Green water puckers my pine hull.
I sit in puddles of blue wine and vomit, indifferent
To the loss of my anchor and ship's soul.

And now I bathe in the waves of a poem,
Riveted to the stars by the seams of my jeans.
I stand in the jaws of the sky, all alone,
And search for my drowned inner steam,

Where suddenly a blue tint washes away the night sky,
And hallucinations rhyme within my head, and slow the rotations of my neck.
Strong alcohol clouds a musical eye,
And makes the bitter red nipples of love stand erect!

I've seen the sky spit lightning, and I've seen the current dance off breakers.
I know the night and all its laws.
I've seen the dawn fly upwards like a flock of doves,
And I've seen what other men have only wished they saw!

I saw the mystical sun set,
Like an inverted flower, exposing purple roots.
The sea tossed about, as the play changed its set.
The rolling waves, like shivering shutters, gave shaky salutes.

I dreamed of green snow dancing in throngs,
Like the kiss of the sea on shallow shale,
Rhythmically singing phosphorescent songs,
As my timber bore sap, yellow and stale.

I followed, the months, like roaming cattle,
Hysterically redressing my stormy wound.
Mary's feet were in a crater saddle,
As she muzzled the sea by riding the moon.

I slapped the forget-me-not blossoms—
They shivered like the pink eyes of panthers, and made my skin crawl.
A rainbow stood as the sun's tender bride,
And slipped beneath a wave, the crystal sea's only flaw.

I saw the enormous fomenting of the sea's wicker baskets,
Where whales were rotting in its cane claws.
Beached water was stranded in the mouths of barnacles,
As a waterfall urinated into a gulf's hungry jaws

Glaciers, in the golden sun, float like pearls in a paradise of red-hot ash.
Where they seed the ground: bays bloom,
Snakes shed lice in brown grass,
And twist their scales around trees, that reek of cheap perfume.

I would rid the children of their guilt,
And show them golden fish that sing,
About how the froth of flowers can make my roots wilt,
As my seeds fly on the wind's silken wings.

Sometimes, I drift through this badland of blue, in search of a pole.
I gently roll upon this sobbing sea.
Like a flower in the wind, I bend and grow,
As I sit upon the ocean's bouncing knee . . .

Hardly an island, I toss about on my boat's rail,
As screaming sea birds drop white dust in my eyes.
All my canvas lines stand frail,
As drowned men sink slowly, staring at the sky.

Now I, a floating bottle without a note,
Watching the birds cut through the etherized clouds.
All the Hanses merchants gave up hope,
As I sailed by, drunk, wrapped in the sea's salty shroud.

Free, I bob in a foggy violet wake,
And watch lichens of rust pull fingers of fire out of a deep sleep.
I dine on poems sweeter than jam,
As the azure sky washes the morning sun's feet.

The morning haze catches the running colors of the pale moon,
And women ride black seahorses on currents of trouble.
August fishes off July's pontoons,
As the deep blue sky pushes fire down autumn's funnel.

I tremble, from the stench of giants,
Who lurk in the ruts of whirlpools,
And rip stitches out of the calm blue.
I regret the ancient stone and mortar of Europe's tyrants.

I have seen the islands of the night,
And have watched their glittering palms sway and entwine.
I felt free, and had an appetite.
To pick the sparkling grapes, of our future's wine.

True, I've cried a lot, my dawns have been glazed with rain.
After all, the moonlight is only the reflection of the sun's frozen tears.
Love, to me tastes sour—my swollen lips are to blame.
O let my keel splinter! O how I clutch to invisible piers!

If I wanted to taste Europe's water, it would be from a cool spring brook,
Where babies bathe under waterfalls and rinse their locks in its swirling suds,
Where ripples would dance through the water,
As the May air pulls crumbled leaves from buds.

I've sat like a buoy in your sea,
I've been dunked many times by your ships, which row by faster and faster!
I could never uncross your royal arms,
Or escape from the eyes of your hungry slave masters.

—Adapted from Rimbaud's 'Le Bateau Ivre'

Claudia Lapp

HORSES

1
o we must have a lot of horse in us
my forelock swung in my eyes my neck arched
a lot of wild horse in us
i flim from rump of galloping horse over his head i soar
to have to have all these stampeding hoof dreams
there shook hooves and hooves and hooves of horses
foaming skin in thund'ring street dreams
stampeding in air how they shine thru torrential space
wild horse eyes and dreams of gettaway
our horses battered their stalls their eyes jerked white
down main street to the sea
wild wild horses couldnt keep me away
how we love the horse words—pivot of heels and knees!
heads and muscles insistent their trembling seizes us
the horses are outing, pent up no more

2
in the oldtimes we praised epona.
i remember.
we didnt have to dream horse

it is said that
soon the steel fences will not matter
nightmares will be forgotten
rhythm will be restored
we will canter our horses into the sun
the thunder in the ground not be nameless
we will know again what we praise

3
in dreams the world alters

we dreamlink horse and swan
what meaning white mammal/white bird joined?
i stood as horse and floated as swan
indream lila black as night

gives me silver horseswan for my neck
for my throat to sing svanati, it sounds
voice to sound the song that brakes the mane of wild horses

becoming rider i can ride my horse
into the light of day
from night shores where i used to witness horse gone wild
riderless riderless
into darkness that was avalanching to horses
but now i
am the arrow
. . . at one with the drive
into the red
eye, the cauldron of morning
into the light of day we flow

4
the wind has taken me
my shoulders sprouted wings
my vision moves forward
snake shall suck the horse's blood no more
soon the steel fences will not matter
i'll mount the horse skyward, seashore behind me
my impatient body will find its vehicle
like a night army on unstoppable hooves
we, horse-and-i, advance to where the light reassembles

with prism wings
astride stallions of air
we'll bring down light that penetrates
wearing beads of crystal
on horses with crystal eyes
wired to the power center
riding horse power
without bridle astride the good power

exactly the horse i am
devoted and powerful

5
we'll ride the devoted steed
his power felt beneath our thighs
he nickers softly into purple dusk
his tail alive nerve plumage

and the stars come out
and our earantennae
and our nostril chalices
and our temple ears
and our eye orbs connect to the radiance

how good to clop over soft forest earth
our feet drawn down to earth pores
our nerves luminous tuned to a high octave
your mane a wind harp, horse
on the hill let us stand
in ceremony letting sounds play us
on the beach too, symphony
amber shines in the sand
the whales sing and we receive it

6
horse, i'll not make you dance pretty trick steps
but let you trot as you will
reined by master reins
you'll have a precise and ordered gait, horse
enough to make even the tough ones stop, horse
to remember rhythm, beauty and its source

a new radiation, released by horses
is implanted at the centre of persons, earthwide

PARTNERSHIP DREAM

a familiar building is being demolished
it falls very slowly with no sound
the dust settles, empty sky
and yet
a building is still there
only more space now
the demolition crew who wear golden hats
are bringing down debris thru gold tubing

you insist on mowing the lawn
with a hand mower

in the garden that surrounds the fallen
still-standing walls
i'm afraid you'll hit chunks of metal or glass
but you go on mowing

among young greenery by the fence
i find an iridescent indigo bird's egg

DIGGING

this rage to dig self
dig up self
get to the bottom of it

i try anything for revelation
    palmistry
      psychodrama
i'm remembering
    how mad i got when they cut my hair
    how i broke a window, said it wasn't me
    how i lorded it over the kids on the block
    how i hated my dolls, mutilated them
    how i loved to be tied up and rolled in blankets
    how the smell of blankets drove me wild

Irving Layton

FLORIDA NIGHTS

Cavafy's poems fill me with compassion, envy;
dead, he no longer suffers his greatness.
A mysterious illness keeps me in bed.

My lover has returned sullen;
beautiful, yes, but sullen.
Black clouds squeeze the light from the sky.

The household god announces
the usual proscription lists,
the names changed to make them interesting.

A visiting madman swears to his wife
to live guided by prudence and moderation.
Caesar is dead! Long live Caesar!

Insane chatter. An evening of turpitude
lies on my empty plate
like a bone whose marrow has been sucked dry.

Beyond the curtains, the lake is a slain leviathan
peacefully laid out between
the tall white candles at either end.

Illusion! The night is alive with insects;
long carbeams knife into the dark
that bleeds drop after drop into the distant valley.

Restless from pain, I sit on the balcony alone.
O prophets O saints, from where shall come
the mastering strength for the chaos within?

RUNCIBLE
For Linda Sobel Halbert

My cat Runcible I call her
Her Greyness because she's all grey
outside and inside as well I guess
A long thin streak of misery
with a brush-cut from tail to nose, no kidding
I never saw a cat so discontented
in all my life so displeased with everything
shrilling her meows of disapproval
from the minute I open the door
and she hulks sulks slouches greyly wanly
to the bowl filled with cat food
I tell my wife never to buy it's so expensive
and anyhow doesn't bring a single thankful purr
from Her Greyness turning up her whiskers
and meowing disdainfully but just the same
keeping her nose in the bowl and chewing away
You may ask why do I keep her
when my wife is all for drowning her
or driving that unneutered nastiness
into the streets she's so irritated
by the cat's constant fussiness
like that of a valetudinarian
nothing will put into a good humour
not even the thrilling news that a cure
has at last been found for cancer
Why *do* I hang on to her? I guess it's because
I like anything that's pure unmixed extreme
and her feline sourness is so complete
an old curmudgeon would die of envy
seeing how she exhibits it over choice ground meat
or a saucer full of fresh cream
that I place in front of her twitchy nose
to see how far she'll take her disapproval
of a world she never asked to be littered in,
her dislike of it so absolute
there's an unmistakable hint of greatness in it

Also she does remind me of my dead mother
and of certain other people whose names
are in my diaries 1943-1976
and anyway my two favourite ancients
honoured above all others, Homer himself,
have always been Archilochus and Thersites
two Greeks who bitched themselves into immortality

BRIEF LETTER TO CERVANTES

I told the dark noble-looking Spaniard
behind the counter
I wanted nineteen pesetas of Gouda cheese
—they were all I had

With proud Spanish courtesy
he knifed through the pale-yellow cheese
and put the two thin slices
on the scale

Ah, too much, by one peseta!

I waited smilingly
for him to say, "Here, take them
and God be with you"

Instead he angrily flung the pesetas
back at me as if each coin
was a scrounging offensive little bastard
and I father of them all

The noble Castilian was outraged;
mad, as if I'd tried to trick him
into a kindness

That, Cervantes, was your countryman:
no wonder, famous and read by everyone
you froze and starved

THE HIGH COST OF LIVING

I sprawl like a naked whore;
the world's infamies fall away:
its pageload of murders, assassinations,
political lunacies. I swear
I'm done forever with chronicling
the antics of a demented ape
who finding hate energizes more than love
crimsons the ground he walks on
and couples one pool of gore to another
till this magnificent and various planet
submerged under an ocean of blood
shall become a painted glare beneath the sun.

Nothing may cross the Maginot Line
I've erected of tall celery;
each stipe stands like a green sentinel
asking the rough breeze
the day's password
while a robin tugs away
as if my small toe was a worm
or hops between my outstretched legs
as if he had invented
a solitary game for himself
to exhibit for my admiring eyes
the radiance of his small and perfect life.

I feel I'm turning into a celery stalk;
my limbs feel lighter than leaves.
Insects that have commerce with me
buzz me from time to time
to get my bearings
or cavort on gorgeous wings,
making a thoughtless tumult
to deepen the silence around me.
Neighbours, when my spouse returns
tell her I've flown off with the boldest
to see what can be done
about the high cost of living in America.

GREETINGS

The black squirrel
in the tree,
jumping from arm to arm
pulls the sunlight after him
before hiding in a cleft
where his long agitated tail
is the day's
golden tongue greeting me

Ross Leckie

BROKEN SPRING

I hear the sound of hands clapping and
I see Jenny down in the yard
a child applauding the air or perhaps
the somnolent crows in the aging elm
From my upstairs window
I am aware of distances
     How young I felt in brisk autumn
     Hands cupping the plump fullness of a football
But things are breaking open like my splitting headache
Water tumbles from the roof in long icicles
Sap drips from a slit maple branch
The hulking form of the old sofa
     put out there for broken springs
reappears wet forlorn from the soiled snow
I step back from the window
for a diminishing view
In the thaw
of this season
old wounds are reopened

A SCARRED LANDSCAPE

Mr. Pit is old now and
tired of selling real estate
He longs to bike to Tierra del Fuego
feel his hair flame to the wind

His first wife is a memory flower
He desires passionate women
discovers them along the roads like crushed stone
They have never seen a motorcycle

Marguerita has that charred complexion
which ignites fields of his love with fireweed
He finds the open book of her heart
is a lecture in Latin American history

He has brought a Marguerita home with him
momento of a fiery dream
He speaks Spanish almost well enough to put a spell on time
Time which is a carbon dioxide foam in his veins

III

Stepping out of the bush into a clearing
I come upon the bus, idling. A gentle
horse, his sad smile in a grill, the ticking
wipers wipe a tear from his eye.
I creep lightly through the snow, whisper
in his rear-view mirror. He shivers
with the stampede of intentions. Rivers and streams
we discover, a network of streets. We flash
by a forest of telegraph poles, shudder at the awesome
mountainous skyscrapers. We pale at the expanse
of a parking lot. My sad creature shakes a wispy
tail of smoke. He whinnies a sigh of regret.
I dismount and he stamps a foot as if to say
'watch your step'. We stand on a large blank lake.
I drift into the night sky, that vast continental shelf.
I leave the poor beast murmuring to himself.

Carole H. Leckner

WHALE SONG, I

The sun catches its glints off the whale's back
      rolling in the sun
            black in the waves
The sun is orange in the dawning sky
The air is crisp with the rising sun.

I am in my boat, waiting with my harpoon.
I am calm. I wait with my spear.
The light grows off the whale's back.
The time comes, the time now.
The sound of the sea says, Move, Hungry One.
The sound of the whale laughing
Calls my spear to leave my hand,
Calls my eyes to see only the whale's brow
As it furrows in waves like the sea.
The whale laughs at me. It is not afraid to die.
He swims around my boat.
I am cool in the newly risen sun
Which beats against my back like his stare.
He will die now.
The spears leave my hand one by one.
He fights, but he laughs
And dies.

I pull him to the settlement with my own hands
To share his meat and fat with my family.
It is good to have killed the whale.
I was not afraid for him to kill me.
But my family would not have had whalemeat
And all the men before me died.

ENERGY AND APPEARANCES

i
When hair is combed
it is as though
nothing happened

ii
When the hair is dyed with henna
it glows and signals
the red flower heart

iii
When the molecules separate
the energy shoots a stream in the air

Stephen Luxton

LOONY TUNE

Spring nights now and the moon's
close-up,
a table top of illuminated crystal on which nature has unfolded
intricate blue prints.
No more winter brownstudies then, but spring moonstudies!
Pay attention if body and soul hanker
for a little animation,
a little post-winter concert
...some chin up, eyes bright, April boogie....

Oh lovely spring logo!
:moon:
summoner all day these days and nights too—
through the dark crowds of matter in each
of our billion cells,
little nucleic lunes pop up like applause signs;
you performer all beings on this earth resound
in croonfilled feisty orbit around.
Oh warm-up comedian, cartoon character, all
of us get the joke,
applaud and love your subtle silver engagement.
We all worship your bouncing silver ball
and sing en masse along
doing nature's fresh work
with Nature's worksong,
throbbing out the measures on uninhabitable
procreation.

Rollicking opening chords: round
the sprouting bulbs of wild leaks,
nightcrawlers at twilight glimpse that gay silver light
high at the end of their tunnels.
They put on tuxedos of their best dark slime,
set out on the long undulant climb
after alchemical moonness.
Nocturnals turn out of their soilsacks:

porcupines shuffle up the trick stairs of woodpiles
to grab a peek from the peak
while their quills blurr and twitch like showgirl plumes
when shimmers of moonlight
sprinkle into the dressing room.
And smelt, thronging in the estuaries of brooks,
jostle off their cabin fever,
hallucinate on their bellies the smooth touch
of buckshot gravel at the heads of feeder streams.
They flutter their fins and by the millions are away!
May they make it in numbers past the nets;
in fever, millions gliding past winnowing frets!
For when spring is trial, you, moon, also offer consolation.
You assure the fish that whatever comes to pass,
one great cosmic egg is lodged safe
in the riverbottom sky
—you assure old hubby January, cuckolded
by his disco-baby, May, that there exists
a constant symbol of inconstancy bringing him comfort,
—you assure an aging beauty
(who took insufficient note of pastor Herrick's sermon on the
    ephemerality of roses)
that, fueled by unconsumable wisdom, she might still retain
the better part of the fire
—you footnote the quivering yellow fingernails of old men,
ten lunicules that say: look here!
death has always peeked out at you,
he does no more than that today
—you arrest the raw and brutal youth
by pointing him to your abraded skull at the top of the sky
and say, *now* go seek your proper relation and level!
For new though venerable moon, yours is a shrivelled and lunar aspect.
Vitae brevis, lunus longus; I expect
you got those blue varicose veins and cellulite
from standing on your feet too long
rocking the world's cradle just as Whitman surmised
—quickening and sobering alike all things: virginal Great Lake shore,
suburban dog stare, bumpershine of city councillor's Lincoln Continental,
and, last but not least, poet's trope
—and the brain of the poor poet striving for it,
yearning to go shore on you
to parse first hand starshine in your wrinkles,

knowing all along he never shall, but fully compensated despite,
for the moment his language arrives, it's off again like a rocket
for bright gas clouds and starscapes beyond:
the other stanzas of this looney sprinkle.

So love of mine, Big Momma Lou, it's spring and you're queen of the ball.
Enough with poetry: let's make *compulsive* boogie
to supralunary rhythm-and-blues hits
—telescope our crazy legs in and out
while you, big D.J. in the sky, enjoying a glamorous three-quarter-shadow
      profile,
spin your gold disc over and over again: moonrock.
Let's roll into the Funkey Turkey, necks outstretched, heads up, beaks
      open to drown in moonspray,
let's be loosed, singing in sprung rhythm, with the billion smelt
      bayonetting up streams
let us ravel like worms, sprawling in the twinkling dew, our six hearts
beating in perfect harmony, our opposite orifices crooning hermaphroditic
      junetunes to ourselves,
let's talk Mr and Mrs Porcupine out of their panoply, persuade them to
      take up weaving headbands for their friends,
sure, let's scribble verses, each word shining like the hub caps of Buicks
      lined up in Lovers' Lane,
let's animate: let's wax to the Sylvester Cat up above, fleeing the big
      bloated bulldog of a cloud,
all of us now, let's congregate, significate, let's loony tune,
—in a landscape pulsating like a Saturday night crowd at the bandshell,
we'll collide and pursue each other,
we'll howl, scramble madly, light the dynamite stowed in our pants, make love,
we'll belt out of the hollow log of our winter selves off the proverbial cliff
      and plummet giggling straight up in the air
(say, that's one up on roadrunner!)
while birds grin and whistle Shostakovitch, we'll rave out all this jazz....

Keitha MacIntosh

STEPHEN'S DAY

Stephen,
      we walked
            through sowed fields
holding hearts
      though words
      were a fence
      between us
In the barnyard
            we found the heifer
            had calved
            She stood
            blood-spattered, worn
            her weariness
            holding her,
            still
The wet calf
      trembled
      fearful of new entries
      holding itself
      A foetus still
You were silent
      surprised
            watching
            your first
            newness
(Stephen, I watch your newness. Remembering.
Days passed me while I hesitated, waiting for signs.)

On the ridge   you said:
            this rock
            is old
            as the earth
(Stephen, how old is old? How can we know? Who
gives us the news?)

We touched rock moss
        soft green
        and caught its
        deep old currents
        to store against
        uncertain days
        of drought
A hawk arced over us
        a partridge flurried
        into pine

We chose two paths
        through cedars
        returning

In the yard
        calf shivered
        thrusting out legs
        drawing them in
        rejecting
        dependency
on earth
    pelt drying
    to vibrant red-brown
Heifer stood apart
    torn by new rituals
    Unprepared
    for violent
    awakenings
(Stephen, are not we always
        unprepared?)

We moved through buckwheat
        that closed around us
        quilting us
        on green and white patches
        determining
        our position
Log house waits
    smoke wakening
    anticipation
    of cedar wood
    aromatic

              sending out vibrant
              messages
Words are a blanket
              spread out
              between us
We are comforted
              by warm
              bread smells
              and let flame
              hide our knowing
              of separate paths

Avrum Malus

NO COMPASSION

We will be ruthless
the ceremony takes a cutting away
no compassion
it is the only way we can get on with the things we must do now
such as repair our marriages
save our businesses from bankruptcy
have our babies
do our work

all it takes
is the ceremony of cutting away

no compassion

"The fledgling swallows high up in the attic"

The fledgling swallows high up in the attic
squee squee squee
(is Julie here this morning or is this marriage broken?)

The swallows will squee squee squee
every summer
whether or not this marriage survives

John McAuley

THE BED IS ITALY IN MOTION

the bed is italy in motion
the bed is a peninsula of golden bells
the pillows are seven hills of feathers
from the bird of paradise

the bed is moving like a little dog
rolling on its back
the lovely lady's tongue lowers like a bucket
into the length of the room

a moth has found entrance &
presses against all of the walls
wrought with religious medals &
flickering candles & soon
the moth is painted in flames

the man's rhythm is slow
as a pendulum in a grandfather clock
the man is bending over
the way italy divides the mediterranean
sicilian to boot

what a way to grow

Creation

is a licensed trademark

THE ENTERTAINMENT OF TOURISTS IS
THE BUSINESS OF THE PLACE

The James brothers from Philadelphia, at the seashore
of Atlantic City stand with straw hats & rolled up pants
in pliant ripples watching Pierrot strum a banjo
singing about the execution of his heart.
"Sow a character," says William, "& you reap a destiny."
Henry nods: the idea for Daisy Miller takes the form
of the ocean, his eyes outstare the waves
searching impatiently for a sign of rescue
from the summer rites of enforced idleness,
knowing his thinking machine has gone out
on the longshore current beyond the hooks & tires
of barrel chested lifeguards & police; he fears
William is a covert pagan, a seeker of clumsy signs
concerning man's behaviour & he fears the oracular cell,
the silent protobion. As the gulls call & call
the history of narration begins.

Robert McGee

REBUKE

(a memo to the beaver)

*We read of the beaver that when it is pursued, knowing
that it is for the virtue (contained) in its medicinal
testicles and not being able to escape, it stops: and to be
at peace with its pursuers, it bites off its testicles with its
sharp teeth, and leaves them to its enemies.*

                                                Leonardo da Vinci

White on the ice a blank pap
your lodge of mud and nerve endings
empty now of relentless tools
the tombstone teeth they kicked
from your jaw's chainsaw
hang strung about my lady's breast

You thought they came for fur
we smelled your fear downwind
coupled on your still-warm hide
where you left it with the balls
you bit off cornered
and it wasn't your medicine they wanted

O national eunuch

Your fear of the Cree nothing
Choking broken in a snare nothing
Twin crossed assholes for eyes nothing
Blanket of ice pulled over you nothing
Skinned with a black bear's femur nothing
Pelt strung to a stretcher nothing
Combed of vermin by the women nothing
Body boiling ugly in a pot nothing
Hard bones thrown to the river nothing
Blackjack tail still twitching nothing
Lake bottoms minus your language nothing

Compared to this dam they're building
an imitation of your blind design
O beaver

THE OTTER

for Edward Tapiatik

Forget the seventh dike
just ignore the grunts of machinery
grubbing for blackspruce roots
just tell me about when
the otter was that big

Forget the entire night-shift summer
all those spot-lit circles of hard clay
we chipped down to lunar bedrock
just tell me about the otter
sleeping under the moon

Forget the hand-held hurricane
like Aeolus' bag of compressed air
tearing off the rug of soil
blowing out of control all night
just imitate the otter's whistle

Forget the rising sun held hostage
in a tangle of blackspruce
desperate for its release
tell me again why two moose
trapped the otter in an antler cage

Just tell me why the animals met
and decided to drown their prisoner
tell me again how surprised they were
to see the otter swim so well
so black in white water.

CROMLECH

A cromlech, or dolmen, is the simplest form of megalithic tomb, consisting of a large capstone and three or more supporting uprights. The ancient Irish believed it to be an entrance to the otherworld, as well as a dwelling place for the dead and a retreat for dispossessed gods. It is said that oracular utterances were often given warriors and druids from its portal. North-west of Mullinavat, County Kilkenny, in Ireland, lies a very large cromlech. "Leac an scail' (flagstone of the warrior).

The Berkshire Horse, a large chalk figure 360 feet long from head to tail, was carved on a hillside near Uffington, Berkshire, in Britain, by a Celtic tribe, the Belgae, some 2000 years ago.

1

There was this big wind
for weeks pulling huge oaks
like rhubarb out of Ireland
kept fishermen with their peat-fire wives
kept pigeons from their industry

'Tea & Snacks' kept me
defiant of the storm's ridicule
while across the Kilkenny road
it made away with several kegs
of Guinness as a lorrie unloaded

From there the pilgrim miles led
through a valley shattered into fields
bordered with piled stones

I managed all the obvious rock
and occasional earth
with a meat and bone bargain
the damp not helping my knee any

Moon rising at arm's length
summoned up conspiracies
cattle straying all over the road

a rabbit driven from its burrow
something like milk
pouring out of its eyes

2

There this man stopped for me
sickle on the front seat

His mouth a ditch around
the ruined abbeys of his teeth

Shoulderblades the wooden wings
of a hump behind his neck

And the death that gnarled
this character with oak hands

Glared from the rear-view mirror
when he let me off

That same death worked diligently
at an old man hardly visible

In the rain near Kilmogue
shoes muddy from the field

Earth sucking at his cane
he burst through the hedge

Ancient scratched and inquisitive
and pointed out the way to the cromlech

3

The only approach through a farm
buildings in a ringfort
in a circle for protection
the dog barking and dancing damp

Eyeing me from the stable door
a woman emerged
in a dung-smeared apron
with red cheeks she walked
around the tractor
Berkshire Horse on the fender
Stonehenge on her boots
and her teeth in the house

She showed me the margin
of trees surrounding it
you could see the end
of the capstone pointing east
hear a stream beyond the trees

The long unhewn slab wedged
onto four other stouter ones
overgrown with moss   '
an aching molar
stuck fast to the county's jaw

4

So I pitched my tent
in the night-shift of earth
put out the candle in my cup
while wind's army roamed murderous
with a throat full of thunder

Plowing hillsides its chariots
and infantry trampling cabbage
tore up my tent's safe cell

Drove me into the cromlech
just inside the portal mouth
knees to my shoulder cringed
squatting solid in the siege

The cromlech withstood

Its shale haunches and thick spine
kept me from the subversive wind

5

I was given no utterance
no tomb secrets no oracle
just this stone she-wolf

Who suckled the voice
I fought back the black
night's babel with

No bearded omen
to curb the world's wind
but strangely lucid

When morning finally came
and I could see my hands
I left for New Ross

Anne McLean

RESCUE

Once a man came over the falls in a boat,
his outboard motor gone, his dog drowned,
no oars or even a paddle left.
Now it had disarmed him, the river
played with him, passing him round
like a driftwood stick, from eddy to eddy.

My father had been putting his tools in for the winter,
preparing the house for a 6-month absence, mending
screens, his mind on the long drive south.
But something made him look up at just the moment
when the boat and the man skimmed down for a landing.

My father took the seven-horse and a good thick rope,
and coming alongside was surprised to find
a man he'd known from boyhood. What a talk
they had that afternoon, laughing as they climbed
the rough shore in the long, late shadow of the old pine.

That man was dead—crushed by a speeding truck
three months later to the day
when he stepped out to check his tires
on a lumber company road half a mile away.
And my father of a heart attack in a southern resort town.

A HUNTING SONG

A hunter came down from the north
With his gun so black and narrow
And the shadow fell on the fallen snow
And the starlight on the barrel.

And the green moss cried from the tree:
What is your purpose, man, what your deed?
'O, I am tracking down a little deer,
The one true love of my life long need.'

O hunter, hunter, the wind blows cold,
The moon drags low on the water,
And her tracks in the snow are tiny hearts
That lead where no man may enter.

But here is the keeper of the frozen glade
And here is the fixer of the hours
Who wears a sign on his forehead
And watches from the tower.

Whose blood is a window, and bone the door,
And the skin of a bear for his bower
And the crow that feeds on the winter corn
Wings sharp above his tower

'O keeper of the frozen glade,
Give me favour, grant me shelter.
I'm a hunter lost in the deep bright snow.
Help me find my own true lover.'

Poor hunter, killing is your destiny
For killing is your duty
And her heart was made for your bullet, placed
Like a target in her body.

You may lie with her one cold night long.
May you find some comfort in the dreaming.
She's made you a nest in her soft breast
Where all her life blood's streaming.

Then take her horns for a trophy
And carve her bones for the marrow
And depart from her by the word of Law
That was written down before you.

So he took her horns for a trophy
And he carved her bones for the marrow
And deep his tracks and his gun so black
And the starlight on the barrel.

THE BIRTH OF THE HORSE

A bright shape fell into the ocean from the sky. Swimmers struck out from the island after dark. Searching for a meteor, instead they found the horse.

Among them, with ropes, they dragged the white animal out of the coloured sea, and left it tied, struggling in the unbearable air through the night.

Coiled in delirium it sang songs from the depths, and sank into sleep like a white parachutist in a skintight costume.

But the divers and nightwatchers were not tricked by this false death. At the first ray of dawn, when the village woke, they came and pressed their lips to its ears like horns.

Its aqua eyes blossomed then, twin morning glories, and for the momentous opening a great crowd filled the beach, but the horse only gazed on them as if on its own children.

Such a creature of waves seemed perfectly born to spectacle. Promoters ganged and parleyed. Some wanted to convince the horse to stand in the public square and be a monument for the town, like the first steam engine. Others searched for wings along the seams of flank and shoulder.

The horse's fins still flexed as it floundered on its side, but now every breath had to be torn from the air. The time for hope and novelty was madly running out. Miracles burst in heart after heart.

Crowds ebbed and soon the beach was empty but for the ones who craved sheer craving. Lurking like sullen outcasts, hands in pockets, eyes averted, they nudged one another forward to a distance of some yards. There they stopped and swayed. In their strangely quiet hearts it was the hush before a daring circus act.

They cut the clear nylon cords, for a laugh, retreating a small way back for safety's sake. When nothing moved they came closer, linking arms like shy people with the sun in their eyes, standing for a photograph. And froze that way for hours, transfixed and satisfied to be looked at in return.

Then the horse stood up, as if its bones would break, and died for them only with a bow and a fall.

FOUR WINDS

The heart has its four winds
And feeling is one
As the east wind brings rain
Blows a while but gives none

The north wind brings dreams
And puts frost in the heart
And the dark night unending
And death has its part

In the howl of the night
And the tower of the gale
The heart turns a season
And the west fills the sail

But the heart has four winds
And it calls to the last
And the south sends the fire
And the earth-shaking blast

O the heart has its four winds
And their time comes again
In this valley of sorrows
On Gaza's broad plain

Mary Melfi

HERE IN MY ARMS

It's better than holding a telephone
or a microphone in my hand,
much better than holding a pair of sunglasses
or holding a grocery bag in my arms.
It's even better than clutching
a purse stuffed with diamonds and pearls
because that's comfort
and comfort isn't more alive than I am,—like sawdust.
This is alive. This is my baby and I need her to be here in my arms.

WELCOME

My house is more important than my hair.
Here take my hair. Make a harp out of it.
My own delicious house remains over my bald head.

When all my friends have plotted to execute me
(as a snowman is executed) outside their houses
my own house will remember me.
My house, my country, will come and take me away.

Once outside their crazy borders
with or without a wig, my house, my hero,
will let my body pass through it like a comb.

Stephen Morrissey

THE TREES OF UNKNOWING

it is 3AM & the house is silent
the piece of fir tree

beside me
is better than any incense

or the smell
of any flower

my friends are scattered
across the earth   one in

spain others in england
if we cld return to switzerland

or italy & live together
or if you & I cld go to

a white house in nova scotia
& wait for them   wd they ever come?

or we can replace waiting
with watching the snow

that now covers the grass & beach
& moves down to the ocean

where the water
melts the snow & the pebbles

& stones are washt & moved
almost imperceptible distances by the waves

until the whole earth
is a movement of waves & stones

moving & being scattered & broken
into sand & dust

the mind is like a tree
that has lost every leaf

there is a tree I pass
everyday

& tonite the moon
was behind it & the branches

were an austere & silent darkness
juxtaposed against the nite sky

the only sound
the rain against the window

and tomorrow there will be
a blue sky of unknowing

& in the sky there are trees
& they are trees of unknowing

there is less we can be
sure abt   less everyday the

things we can
know for certain

the seagulls leave
their footprints in the snow

everyday they come & eat
whatever is left for them

WAVES

between waves
there is a moment of silence

a wave that stretches a hundred feet
along the shore & which suddenly collapses

the lip of the wave turning over

until the whole wave is a white cap
& then noise & finally

a bit of white foam at your feet

on the pier in ventura
were dehydrated starfish

their legs hanging lifeless
where they were placed

china is not far away
& behind us is the east & to the right

the north stretches along the coast
a two thousand mile long series of waves

being alive is to ride the waves
and not get washt up on a deserted beach

or sacrifice one's life to the meaningless
efforts of swimming against the current

we dont want tidal waves crashing against our backs

being alive is to ride the waves
with one ear between crest & trough

& the other to the imperceptible
discussion of fish & shells & rock

POEM

I lie upon you
as tho you were a warm

beach & your arms
the sun on my back

your breathing
is the sea

& I walk along the beach
picking up shells &

smooth stones
which I return to you as presents

and when you take my hand
& when you

hold me
it is like finding

a gold doubloon
in the sand

I hold it
as tho it were the sun

that was burning holes
through the palms of my hands

Henry Moscovitch

UNTITLED

I train myself to
write almost daily.
I eat my bacon and eggs.
I invest in the lottery.
I dress warm when it rains.
I put on my overshoes
for the snow.
I live in a lonely room
where I awake
from my dreams of you.

UNTITLED

I wait for
the fall,
the fall of civilizations
so I can
build my nest
in their embers
and record
for the visiting
gods
the ruin.
Still all things
endure.
The great men
will return,
I promise myself
before I go to sleep.

UNTITLED

I reached into my
pocket
and found
a song to spare.
I gave it to you
at night
with all the stars
as witnesses.
Now my song
flutters like a banner
and all your
faces
thank me
in a dream.

UNTITLED

All alone
this cold day,
I hear the
city echo
my thoughts.
I am trapped
in a vase.
I will never
survive.
But when
spring
comes
like a poem
they will find
me there,
a single snowman
who's endured
the seasons.

Sharon H. Nelson

ANOMALY

we write.   we write
in this strange tongue
but our breathpauses
our natural inclinations to rhythm
are cantatorial.

for in our inner ears
lie foreign sounds:
pause for breath between
one benediction and another
one curse and another:
blood frogs   blood locusts   blood darkness
blood of the firstborn son

between the golem
and the harpist
no song raised itself
but terror

we are left, like moses:
our mouths dry, our tongues swollen,
we seek the perfect line, invent syllables

breathing becomes a parable

GATE

they say
this dream will pass

the dream will not pass

they said
we will light
eternal fires

we will build

a ladder
to god

always the same promethean arrogance
the same burnt-out Icarus
the same wings, the same ladder, the same logic

marching
across Egypt, across Russia
through
Siberian or Sinaian dream

all landscape
the same
to bloody feet

stoned
from village to village
for what sin

who knows why
who even knows
how to ask a question

reassembled finally
at one small Gate

in the end
all corpses will enter
by one small space

there will be room enough
for all of us

this myth does not die

CALIPERS FOR THE MOON

and so
we know
the moon is
black as coal

some nights
the wind blows
i stretch
get tall and rangy

mean and silent
i count my words
each syllable's cost
the price of each
communication

the moon's full
blots the page:
i am skittish

outside a beaver
walks on the verandah
the cat stretches

i hear the beaver crunching branches
building
yet another home

but i am boiling up a poem
restless
verging
on hysteria

i grow mean
and uncommunicative

why does it have to be
like this?

too many cigarettes
the sour taste
the empty bed
tightness in eye-corners
and the inability to concentrate
on any other thing

some men
don't know what i'm talking about

grin broadly
snicker 'menstrual'
and with wide open smiles and eyes
make verses

and speak of love
in the first person
and are heroes always
to themselves

but we
are not
like that

we
are
cold
and dark
and tight

like blackheaded witches
we stalk the night

we who are
cramped
grow

:to be consequential

:to fill up space with our bodies

:to fill up space with poems

Ken Norris

IN THE SUPERMARKET

I am in the supermarket
                surveying
The prospects of the dairy section
When a female hand
                    darts out
Of nowhere
And quickly plucks
         a huge round of Gouda cheese
From the shelf.
I am astounded—
         the cheese is above my means.
I turn to observe
         the face of the fortunate lady
Who can afford such extravagance.
She is a pigtailed beauty
Wrapped in a leather coat.
My emotions rise:
I love her and the cheese.

Quickly she is off, pushing
Her cart before I can say a word.
So I go on shopping.
I cool my passion by perusing
A section of frozen foods.
But later, over turnips, we meet again.
My love grows
Among the fruits and vegetables.
I decide to hold an asparagus
        between my teeth
And dance with the flash of a flamenco;
But she disappears again
After taking advice from a counterman
About raisins.

I go back to my purchasing.
I squeeze a tomato, caress an eggplant,
Get excited about the price of lettuce.
In the bread section I decide
That if we ever meet again
          I will give her a potato
To show my affection.
If she accepts it
          we will stroll through the store,
Our purchases in one mutual cart,
          and sing praises
To the A & P,
          our divine matchmaker.
We will be like apple pie and ice cream,
          pork and beans,
Baked potato and sour cream.
And I came here looking for food!
Bah, mere sustenance!
In this atmosphere of plenty
I have found love!

I remember that she has vanished among the aisles.
I look for her in soups, cereals, salad dressings;
She is not there.
On to meats, cookies, spices;
                         Alas!
In despair
          I decide to check out;
She stands before me,
Emptying her cart out onto the conveyor.
She moves with such grace.
I observe the bounty of her cart.
She has cans of cat food,
A sure sign of loneliness.
Besides the cheese
          which brought her
Into my blood
She has minor items.
She has an eggplant wrapped in cellophane.
My cart contains one too:
A common affinity.
A jar of meat sauce, stewed tomatoes.

She plays with a pigtail as she waits.
The check-out girl is slow.
My love speaks to the girl in the language of the land;
Perhaps they briefly discuss Quebec appetites.

I cannot tell; I am not a delicate crepe
Nor a stocky bouillabaise; I'm an English stew,
Worse than that, American,
A hamburger with french fries and a coke.

My heart sinks.
Her total is soon added,
The items placed in bags.
She pays and turns to leave.
I want to call out to her a recipe,
A helpful hint about spaghetti, anything.

Too late, too late.
All the way home
I long for her company at dinner.

LE BESOIN

You can die of it. Don't think you
Can't. Why just last year I collapsed
Into 14 various fits of depression
Because of it.
It makes no difference what is labeled
Necessity. The things you need are the things
You need. I know a woman who needs
Warm male bodies beside her in bed.
She needs them implicitly. It would
Mean the end were she to awaken at 3 a.m.
And find nothing but dust lying
In the place beside her.

There is, of course, the needle
Filled with refined fruits of the poppy.
Break a junkie's spike and watch as
Humanity abandons him and he becomes some
Thing that could tear the heart
Out of the moon. Never steal
My bottle and shot-glass
Unless you are prepared to see flesh transmute
To liquid before your eyes. The need,
The need. Some need newspapers, some need
Coffee, some need to observe
Others needing. To think you are
Above needing is an act classifiable
As criminally insane. To act as though
You need nothing is normal. But confess,
Confess to yourself as you turn the pages of the paper,
Confess as you pop your morning vitamin pill,
Confess as you cash your biweekly check,
Confess as you watch the Canadiens-Boston game,
Confess as you read your 49th Agatha Christie book,
Confess as you bend to tie your shoelace,
Confess as she's taking off her clothes for you,
Confess to yourself in words that are more
Than silent, that are less than silent,
I need this, I need this, I need this.

ODE
TO THE POSSIBILITIES

It is as if you've just called from the airport,
are on the way in, and it is the right action
taking place in the wrong year.
What we are having for dinner is questionable;
we know that, in part, it will be each other
but what about all those other wonderful and terrible
                                        delicacies?
The banquet is spread as are the sheets
of the bed, and I suppose I could say
something about your legs here. Your hair
is curling around the corners of the world.

I can't help but wonder how it could have happened.
Whatever became of junk and yellow taxicabs?
We both like Italian food but it didn't start or stop there.
It lingered in the doorways of the world
and you have woven and won a garland of my love,
                                        don't ask
how we have come to this, it is you
who are arriving. I look out the window
and the streets are bright with circumstantial lights.

I've walked along the edge of the river
wondering about the catch the small boats bring in
as they tack their way from shore to shore
zig-zagging against the wind. Have they made it
a good time in the clean waters of upriver?
And now the sun as well as wind catches their sails.

What we make of the night
is all so different from what we make of the day.
Dogs in the street are barking as the sun goes down,
the sky is an absence of purple
having lost all desire to be described.
Stars are gathering force at the filling station of eternity
and night brings you returning to me
on feet neither winged nor sandalled
but in simple leather shoes.

It's been a thin line you've walked between
things done in the name of romance
and those in the cause of depravity.

I've heard you question the logic of these systems
maybe once. It appeals to you, the automatic service
of this or that always ringing your doorbell.
You rarely test the temperature of the water,
the texture or the fluidity of anything.
Your body a painter's pallet, dabs of pigment
adorn you. Cavalcades of bells
and mysterious late night calls compose a litany
that somehow sings the praises of you.

AUTOKINESIS

We haven't spoken to each other for years,
But now, sitting in frail wooden chairs
In my apartment, bathed in sunshine,
She cuts right to the core of my life
As she tells me of autokinesis.

A spot of light, projected on the wall
Of a darkening room, will appear,
To the unadjusted eye, to move,
And the movement will prove
Disturbing to the viewer.
If, however, a frame of light
Is projected around the spot of light
The eye will see the spot of light
As stationary.··

When she
        left
                she took
            the frame
And I watched
            that spot
        of light
Bob & weave
        around the
    wall
Like a running heart

Rena Okada

FROM EIGHTEEN SONGS OF A NOMADIC FLUTE

An interpretation of 14th century Chinese scrolls
concerning the capture of a Chinese woman by Mongols

Capture

I
the moon grows round
captured by a hard sky
    as I am taken
    by a strange man
    who smells of wild things
to a land more unfamiliar
each brief day

II
men are lost
    in war
alive or dead
they lose
    and women taken
    to lie beneath
those who kill. heroes.

III
in the time it took
for one snowflake to fall
from sky to earth
    he was gone
    husband, father
    irretrievable

IV
my sons murdered
before my eyes
    let no sigh escape
    no cry of pain
I will die as
flowers die.

V
one tear mistaken
for a drop of rain
    and I am bound
    by rope and heavy hands.

VI
the first night
    I remember
    a husband lost
to this man's sword
    or were there arrows
    flying like savage birds?

captured from life
to death.   grief
protects me as he comes
armed
    I turn my head
    my body no longer
        mine
the harsh ropes, a comfort
a prayer
    I am still
    he groans
    and is gone

and then it comes
the weeping and the sickness
my body rebels. oh that I were
a man. either death or revenge
both simple acts.

THE McCONNELL SEED CATALOGUE
for Janet Kask

In January, the mail brings a seed
catalogue, true harbinger of spring

I am lost, hypnotized by flowers

Who can choose between
    Hawaiian heather
    Amazon lily

Oh McConnell seed catalogue,
mythical land of flowers and
perpetual spring/replete
with possibilities of
    succulent strawberries, snapping
 carrots and cascades of loganberries
the mysteries of Japanese yew and Chinese
evergreen wait to be unveiled

and three generations of McConnells pose
sensible as potatoes
    grandfather founder
    father chairman of the board
    and son the president (could I ask
for his seed?)

Dahlias explode like fireworks
Violets appear tentative and shy

    I look around
no one watching. Lick a page of
bursting berries, sniff a rose in ten varieties

Marc Plourde

BRANCHES

for Marc and Renée Vanasse

At the start of May
the grounds in certain places were still spotted
with snow not yet melted, despite all the rain
and the small road beside the orchard
could not be walked to its end
and we waited.
When stronger sun came
the apple trees were pruned, cut branches
fell everywhere on the ground, into the mud.
My work was to gather them,
I was told they should be heaped into straight rows
crossing the orchard
down the slope—a machine
would come push them away. It took near three days
to do this work; it paid for my keep.
After, I shovelled manure from the stables.
They told me I could do nothing else
having come from the city
and not smart enough, unable to repair fences
or help on the tractor, slow at my task and it seemed
even in the smallest things I failed: I cut my hands
& wrists handling the branches,
the rows I made were not always straight.

A girl also worked in the orchard,
she brought me water once in a wine bottle
and her eldest brother
told me a story he remembered only parts of
from a book; it was
of an old woman some soldiers shot
by mistake: she failed to answer their challenge,
she was deaf. This happened
not far from the orchard he said, in the last

century—and once
we visited the monument that was set
at the roadside, a plaque with her name, almost
hidden in the grass.
May now has nearly ended itself.
I live in the city again; I waste time
while the Greek boy
who lives upstairs is climbing a pole
to repair his mother's clothesline, and one leg
brushes against the branches of a small apple tree,
half its blossoms already fallen.

HARDHEADS

An idea spirals and burrows upward
the field idea in an ear of wheat
the tree idea that becomes a forest
camouflaged in its leaves
and even, even
growing wild, the crabgrass idea

and men held captive will have it
that fine-edged torment, that courageous
craziness sprouting up
and climbing everywhere at once

You can tell by their twisted noggins
and the damned thing
can't be weeded out, strange!
that idea we hardheads have got, O freedom

                    —translated from Gaston Miron

THE OLD WOMAN AND THE SUN

In the park an old woman finds a bench
and waits for her breath:
'my breath is gone' she thinks, 'it's the heat'
and the heat glistens on her face
and rises with the cut-grass smell of the lawn
now the old woman looks at some stones
between her square-toed shoes, she can feel them
with her cane, those white glaring stones
'I wish it were shady here' she thinks
'and that car hadn't knocked the wind out of me
that time like today and made me
almost blind—oh it's hot today!'
and the sun is a red splinter in her chest
she swallows
and it picks a hole there, 'it's the sun'
she thinks, on the warm bench
seeing nothing but glare
white points like prongs on a fork
white stones she can feel them
while the sun has picked her insides
now she is an insect shell held
transparent and sightless
on the sun's breath—'my breath', she thinks

THE SHADOW'S SHADOW

Death will stumble in its final harvest
though now we thrill and bend with life like a last
remaining blade of grass
soon our world will be a bubble suspended in memory

Death will stumble in its final harvest
death that comes with eyes toppling heaven and earth
with little quick jolts shaking gearshift ignition and steering wheels
with little water jets washing the streets clean
with little kayak leaps bounds spins and toboggan somersaults
death, acetylene death's night-lamps exploding

one morning in lilac shells
sparkling and flashing like a speckled trout
death's weather vane rattling in the throat
death that weighs no more than a shadow's shadow
woman O woman little souls little waves little chains of little shatterings
    in my arms
of rustling cigarette paper
of foliage in the spawning of lush pleasures
of sweet fires stretching to the limit's limit

and in the shadow's shadow of each night
to sleep and love still
O sleep
and flower together

—translated from Gaston Miron

Martin Reyto

JENNY WREN

It was a Jenny Wren dream
she was small with a large head
and the rest of her was motley, like
a quilted bird.

I caressed her ruffles in bed, she
looked at me with wide eyes:
you big ox, she said, to do this
as if you were in love.

I am, I said, it's just the strangeness,
the way your neck tapers into
such a fanciful thing, a tiny sweep
of feathers on the pillow, nothing more—

it takes—I'll get
used to it after a while.
and she: as if it weren't you I saw
carousing with the toy dog all afternoon.

yes it was true. but her child and I
chased the leaping stuffed terrier back
into the closet and I was weaving something
straight out of my hands, from nothing

I said 'what am I doing? it's
so strange' and the child came and hugged me
(the strangeness of it
had made me lonely)

whirl went my hands over each other
and out poured an endless stream
of golden yarn
and swirled down in a deep pile on the floor.

CROW

resting, the crow lights
on one tree and the next
and so multiplies

but in flight he divides the sky
into two planes

as an expert draftsman might
with space and two lines
create sky

so the guided certainty
of crow flight.

clouds dense
at the valley's rim

white splinter
of a dead pine

spring creek spreads like mercury
among the reeds
below the hills
and the mercury sky

where cry and silence meet
rain rests on separate leaves
a leaf tips rain to the grass
and beaded cobwebs weave
leaves to each other

in the vanishing recession
of these minute acts of love
among the countless, separate
spirits of the world, the crow
and the space around him
assume each other

cry

spring creek spreads like memory
among the reeds

rain drifts into mist
gradually amazed

Filippo Salvatore

MY PEOPLE

People, my people,
people as dear to me
as the early morning sun.

Rough-faced people,
dark-dressed plumpy women,
men with patched-up trousers
and corn-like hard hands,
mixed up youths, livestock
ready for slaughter in the huge
city sweat-shops, you who long to kiss
and grasp another young body on Saturday
nights and are content by easy
pleasures and volatile emotions;
elders, you who gather by small groups
in the park during the warm, sunny
days to play scopa squabbling in dialect
like old urchins, waiting patiently
for death,
women, men, youths, elders,
you are all people, all my people.

I watch you live every day,
as you wipe your sweaty brow or
as you blow on your frozen fingers,
as you go out early in the morning
with coffee-odouring mouths or
as you chat in the evening in the bus
about the good food waiting for you home.

I see you arrive, work,
hate, love, learn our new life,
I listen unnoticed to your complaints
sitting strung-eared beside you
for you speak always in a low voice,
I hate your meanness, admire
your courage, adore your tenacity.

I am touched, like a sentimental fool,
if I hear you got a letter from Italy
which says grandma is still sick
and the wheat is already being reaped,
if I hear a beautiful baby-boy was
just born and see your young father's
eye glimmer, if I hear you love him,
for the first time, much, oh, so much,
and he is a handsome young man and hard-working too.

It's our little joys, sufferings,
weaknesses, qualities, I hate and love
so much, people, my people,
people as dear to me
as the early morning sun.

Robyn Sarah

BROOM AT TWILIGHT (Another Way of Drowning)

Some climbs end nowhere. Like the unplanned climb
I took this evening.
     I'd gone down the beach
some little way, and though the sun was low,
I thought that it would see me round those rocks
to the next cove, with time enough to watch
the tide come in (and maybe make it back
without getting my feet wet.)
      No such luck—
beyond that stretch, the tide was in already,
and there was nothing to do but climb the cliffs
up to the road, and walk back home that way.

Dark doesn't wait, this time of year. I climbed,
and the sun went down as I went up. Went right on
falling beyond the unseen edge faster
than I could find my holds. (Footholds in clay,
handholds on anchored roots. And all the while
the sky fast darkening out from above.)

     Near water,
the grey hour's luminous. And by the beach
I should have had no trouble finding my way.
Where I came up, though—something blocked the light.
It was the sameness that surprised me.

    Broom:
a forest of it. Higher than my head.
And not in clumps, the way it seems to grow
by day—but in a solid wall. An army
bristling with strange intent. The broom I knew
grew in tall waving tufts like uncut hay

to wade through at high noon. This broom stood up
like earth's raised hackles in the failing light—
a massing of ominous spikes against the sky
and stems that wouldn't give way. I couldn't find
the mouse-paths children make to get to the sea—
but had to plunge (broom closing over me)
into a tangible edgeless element,
banking on where I thought the road must be.

SINKERS

If in sudden and several places the ground
you walked on wore thin, or opened up
clear through to the other side—what then?
I can remember when it did: spring rain
left holes in parking lots—holes full of sky
where clouds bloomed and expanded like the milk in tea.
We liked to stand on the edge of them: look down
at what we knew was up, but might as well
exist below as above us (why not?)—and tease ourselves
with fear of falling in. Of stepping
one step too far, right over the edge and
down, down into sky without end. Only, to try
with just one round-toed rubber boot, was to bend
the window back into water: once wavy,
that sky lost its power to pull us in.

Now rain-pools are just things to walk around
or step over. But to keep the ground
from seeming too sure under us, there are eyes
that open up bottomless as those sky-holes
to catch us in our tracks. And we keep dreaming
of a clean fall through to the other side—
unasked for, with a cushioned landing
and no charge for the ride.

AN INCH OF AIR

She wants to talk, but he
won't have it—talk—just circular
and besides, he's tired. He flicks
the lamp off, making
an end of it. And there they lie
like two cats, back to back,
in a bed too small for them.
In a moment he's under, a boy chasing
apples down a slope, some other boy
launching them down from a tree. But she,
eyes open in the dark, nerves wired,
writhes like a hooked fish on the line
of his breathing—strung in mid-air
till morning, with a quarrel to revive
over breakfast—what kind of a life. She gives
the sheets a yank—they're caught
under him—another tug
frees them, and he snores on,
uncovered. She curls up
like a spring, timed to uncoil
with the first light. And moves
an inch over, to put some token air
between her back and his.

Lazar Sarna

BIRTHDAY LETTER

1

(born)

the wind
restudied its role
in orchestras;

a flock
of pigeon's lungs
watched her window
to see if she were a bird

2

(first birthday)

Under several layers of her thirst
I have hidden,
like an unignited endowment plan
stories of bruises,
fears of different darks, ducks with uninterrupted eyebrows,
claims to a higher purpose.

She recognizes my paternity
through the menu of her face,
our understandings, mutual, derivative,
blanket the prefaces to her sleep;
in a lava of joy
our attempts to establish feeling
strain through her gums

I take for granted her expression
of undigested raisins;
we are
beyond apologies and obligation;
we are too related to be injured.

3

her occasional word falls
like an intense pebble:
witness the plural furrows,
the shards of night
displaced by the marker's impact

her mouth creates
brush and nests
and even moulds
eggs humming with the shiver
of their yoke.

But shadows intrude beyond her volition:
she is, as yet,
incapable of that subtlety

F. R. Scott

ON SAYING GOODBYE TO MY ROOM
IN CHANCELLOR DAY HALL

Rude and rough men are invading my sanctuary.
They are carting away all my books and papers.
My pictures are stacked in an ugly pile in the corner.
    There is murder in my cathedral.

The precious files, filled with yesterday's writing,
The letters from friends long dead, the irreplaceable evidence
Of battles now over, or worse, still in full combat—
    Where are they going? How shall I find them again?

Miserable vandals, stuffing me into your cartons,
This is a functioning office, all things are in order,
Or in that better disorder born of long usage.
    I alone can command it.

I alone know the secret thoughts in these cabinets,
And how the letters relate to the pamphlets in boxes.
I alone know the significance of underlinings
    On the pages read closely.

You scatter these sources abroad, and who then shall use them?
Oh, I am told, they will have a small place in some basement.
Gladly some alien shelves in a distant library
    Will give them safe shelter.

But will there be pictures of J.S. Woodsworth and Coldwell
Above the Supreme Court Reports? The Universal Declaration
Of Human Rights, will it be found hanging
    Near the left-wing manifestos?

And where are the corners to hold all the intimate objects
Gathered over the rich, the incredible years?
The sprig of cedar, the segment of Boulder Dam cable,
The heads of Buddha and Dante, the concretions, the arrow-heads,
    Where, where will they be?

Or the clock that was taken from the 1923 air-cooled Franklin?
The card-board Padlock, a gift from awakened students?
The Oxford oar, the Whitefield Quebec, the Lorcini?
      These cry out my history.

These are all cells to my brain, a part of my total.
Each filament thought feeds them into the process
By which we pursue the absolute truth that eludes us.
      They shared my decisions.

Now they are going, and I stand again on new frontiers.
Forgive this moment of weakness, this backward perspective.
Old baggage, I wish you good-bye and good housing.
      I strip for more climbing.

METRIC BLUES

Mile, gallon and pound
root me in solid ground,
but metre, litre and gram!
Lhude sing goddamm!

      Kill that smile
      you measured mile.
      The metric talon
      's got you, gallon.
      Frown, pound,
      you're quite unsound.

Metre, litre and gram!
Lhude sing goddamm!

      O heck
      gone is the peck.
      Never again
      a chain.
      No more search
      for the tricky perch,
      and the innocent yard
      is barred.

Metre, litre and gram!
Lhude sing goddamm!

Yell and flinch
ell and inch.
Shudder and scram
Rood and drachm.
Poor pole
you've lost your role
and your daily bounce
ounce.
Pints and quarts?
You're torts!

Metre, litre and gram!
Lhude sing goddamm!

Furlongs, fathoms and rods
dead as the old gods.
Not so much as a stone
for an anglophone
alone.

Lhude, lhude sing
goddamm!

CRITIQUE OF POETRY

It is well known that I hate the power of the bourgeois
And the power of the cops and priests
But I hate even more the man who does not hate it
As I do
With all his might.

I spit in the face of the man who is smaller than life
Who of all my poems does not prefer this *Critique of Poetry*.

Paul Eluard 1895-1952
(translated by F.R. Scott)

THIS IS A LAW

Who says Go
When the Green says Go
And who says No
When the Red says No?
Asked I.

I, said the Law,
I say Go
When the Green says Go
And don't you Go
When the Red says No,
Said the Law.

Who are you
To tell me so
To tell me Go
When the Green says Go
And tell me No
When the Red says No?
Asked I.

I am you
Said the Law.

Are you me
As I want to be?
I don't even know
Who you are.

I speak for you
Said the Law.

You speak for me?
Who told you you should?
Who told you you could?
How can this thing be
When I'm not the same as before?

I was made for you
I am made by you
I am human too
So change me if you will
Change the Green to Red
Shoot the ruling class
Stand me on my head
I will not be dead
I'll be telling you Go
I'll be telling you No
For this is a Law
Said the Law.

LANDSCAPE ESTRANGED

The storm raged about
and the snow blew into our breast
right in the breast
crowned with pain-sharp ice
crowned with thorns
love words driven into the brow

great storm before our eyes in a world estranged
every night tore a cry from us
and we grew up in agony
slowly we were aging
and the landscape aged with us   against us

the landscape was no longer the same
the landscape was sombre
the landscape no longer fitted us like a glove
no longer had the colours of our youth
the landscape the beautiful landscape was no longer beautiful
there were no more streams
no more ferns no water
there was nothing left

the landscape had to be remade.

Rolande Giguère
(translated by F.R. Scott)

Daniel Sloate

I HAD MET YOU IN MANY DISGUISES
BEFORE THE LAST MASK FELL

I had met you in many disguises before the last mask fell.

Once you played ship; I walked your bridge; I was our pilot through storms. One day I saw through your seams.

And once you were a house: those slow corridors, the whisper-hung rafters. I was told one day no house stood by the sea when I was away from you.

And then you played flesh: dream creatures, each with the same smile stretched across different bones.

I remember peeling your selves away on a night of mist and music; there was a fire on the hearth; a hasp of thunder in the attic sprang open, undoing wind and times.

I was going through my desk: unwritten Journals, letters from the dead, torn writings, aborted words. And a half-poem by Borges, written by me, long before I read him.

About a man who wished to compass the universe in a poem: every stone, air, atom, all errors, every glory.

I threw the page upon the fire; one line glowed like diamond through the flames: *you will forget the moon.*

My borges-words leapt up the flue, towards the unhasped heavens.

And I discovered what I knew: all your disguises: the ship, the sea-house, ghosts and flesh, the lips of shadow.

They were all you, moon.

David Solway

POEM FOR MY SONS

Sons, I thank you for the dragons in the salad
and for ticklebelly hills when the highway dips
and thank you for a house wallpapered in Picassos
and for those bangabong Elizabethan songs of yours.
Everything about you exhilarates and makes glad—
the Hansel-and-Gretel trail of potato chips,
the missing grail of wine, the rosy watercolored windows,
dosedo of clothes, the Chinese Hebrew on the stairs.
I thank you for making me more afraid
that nature may grow exhausted, or to come to grips
with these declining times, imagination's close,
and the childless marriage with the coming years.
Thank you for the bunk baths and banana bones.
And for the rejuvenating faith in epigones.

DESIDERATA

Scare me, said the crow.
Kick me, said the dog.
Chop me, cried the tree,
down into a log.

Throw me, begged the stone,
as far as you can.
Bite me, said the bone.
Love me, said the man.

THE POWERS OF THE PAWN

The pawns are the soul of chess—Philidor

The king can move a single square
without restrictions made
but once he topples from his place,
no ransom to be paid.

The queen, as you might well expect's
a complicated dame;
she does most anything she wants
and quite controls the game.

The bishop is a sly old fox,
strategically oblique;
if there is trouble on the board
he is not far to seek.

And some are fascinated by
that most eccentric knight
who gallops rather awkwardly
but loves a bloody fight.

The stately rook's a mighty piece
and mainstay of the force;
he'll beat the bishop anytime
and overwhelm the horse.

But never underestimate
the powers of the pawn
who can promote into a queen
and put a kingdom on,

or moving humbly up the board,
killing on the side,
outpriest the priest, and leave the knight
without a horse to ride,

and trip the elevated rook
to bring it crashing down,
and nudge the psychopathic queen
into oblivion,

and stop before great Caesar's throne,
a tiny regicide,
and watch a cornered monarch fall
and ponder how he died.

NOAH

He has a talent for uneasiness,
drinks too much coffee, chooses to rehearse
the nag and riddle of the universe;
he scans the clearest sky for cumulus
to cloud the heart, declares, in self-embrace,
the arch-perfectionist a candidate for grace.

How can he sit at table, and delight
in cream and figs, and smile? He glumly goes
against the bright ideal of repose,
the lesser peace of coasting in the light,
like Noah in his arcane discipline
troubling wife and neighbour with his prophetic din.

Though he may see what others do not see,
poetry's perception without power;
yet he abandons the sufficient hour
of milk and bread and apples from the tree
and dreams the hour the mind will not defraud
as he saws and he hammers, one eye on his god;

He dreams the distant and unplundered sea,
forgets the portrait on the mantlepiece,
the oaken trestle and the bolster-fleece
and all heroic domesticity;
he dreams the world of the kindred ships,
anticipates the pleasures of Apocalypse.

And is it all a figment of the blood—
this famished, unameliorable mind,
this sea-buffeted, salt-encrusted, blind
imagination calling down a flood?
He stacks his eclogues in unpublished heaps,
diviner of a world in which the dreamer reaps.

So let him itch and twitch, a weatherfrog,
and watch his fingers stain with nicotine.
The nervous poet contemplates a green
Sahara, and, when all is night and fog,
the greater peace of sensing in the dark
miraculous mountains for his uncompassed ark.

LINES WRITTEN IN DEJECTION

You stand on the coast between sky and sea
where, by accident or divine decree,
you happen to be living. And you sense
the loneliness of the circumference,
the frontier poetry of the Chinese
borderguard, the complaint of minor keys,
and the lamentation of astronomers
who know the earth peripheral. It occurs
to you that you must look behind your back
for truth or for beauty, or all the slack
Romantic nonsense we can't do without
and can't do anything with. Look about:
the capital of the empire you find
somewhere in the past, no state but that of mind;
the center of the universe is gone
the way of all beliefs; the music's done.

And you know that you are never really here.
You spend the evenings reading Shakespeare
and dreaming of some legendary spa
on the littoral of Bohemia.
You speak to the neighbors in their language,
study their politics and customs, gauge
the depths of their hellenic cunning, style
yourself tourist, poet, suntanned exile,
prophet, drunkard—makes no difference
when you're living on the circumference.
You stand on the coastline, drowning in blue.
Everything is happening behind you.

Lesbos, 1973

Richard Sommer

27 SEPTEMBER

out early morning for t'ai chi
studio floor littered groggy bumble bees
turn on heater start the form

bees wake up   crawl   one takes off
buzzes up at skylight no way out
just light   promise of out   but not

my own selfish reasons scoop
bee onto paper carry outside where
really cold   the bee lies there

sunless concrete too cold legs
move slow t'ai chi dream black gold
who down in middle hot flower

all summer helped our honeysuckle fuck
made honey under eaves in the middle
of summer now where

think maybe in hand warm up
from the kitchen honey to fuel her tank
but i don't take her in my hand

don't get any honey back inside
start again slow waving hands
under skylight Chinese dance

wondering maybe where the hive
maybe she will get there   wherever
room corner another bee slow stir

and another   and another

WINTER SOMETIME

once upon a time a girl with opaque eyes
sat in a room in the middle of winter
drinking tea

and while the girl with opaque eyes sat
in a room in the middle of winter drinking tea
snow whirled against the glass

and while snow whirled against the glass
in a room in the middle of winter a girl
with opaque eyes sat drinking her tea

and while the girl with opaque eyes sat
drinking her tea in the middle of winter
snow whirled against the glass

and while she drank her tea in the middle
of winter the snow whirled against glass
in the room she sat in with opaque eyes

drinking her tea the girl with opaque eyes
whirled snow in the middle of winter
against the glass and sat

and drank her tea in the middle of the winter
while snow whirled against her opaque eyes
in a room of glass in the middle of winter

THE WORD GAME

by this time i am speaking to the reader
who has found his or her way somehow almost
to the end of this book.

anyone else can read this too,
but i am not really talking with them,
i am talking with people

who got here by a beautiful kind of patience
who got here by beautifully understanding
or who got here by a beautiful kind of anger,

listen, i have a suggestion for a game for you.
write a poem in twenty minutes,
like this one was.

don't leave poetry to the poets,
don't try to write a poem,
write one.

just pick up a pencil & write one.

THE CORNERS OF THE MOUTH

the mouth moves noisily in eating.
the lips move heavily in eating.
the teeth move in eating, greasily.
the tongue moves, shaping gobbets.
even the corners of the mouth move,
but they do not move as the others do.
they move only as the hinge of eating.
the corners of the mouth do not eat.
eating needs the corners of the mouth.
eating turns around the corners of the mouth.
eating couldn't do without the corners of the mouth.
nevertheless the corners of the mouth do not eat.
no, the corners of the mouth keep themselves clean.
a napkin helps to keep the corners of the mouth clean.
no grease is allowed to stick in the corners of the mouth.
the corners of the mouth have no need to eat.
eating is done for the corners of the mouth.
the corners of the mouth are without blemish.
the corners of the mouth are blameless.
the corners of the mouth never eat.
it is the others that do the eating.
it is the others that eat.

Ben Soo

THE ALL EDGES BAND
ESTUARY, SIDE TWO
LIZARDS

We bring the hangings down
We bring the blackboard sound
We bring the crocodiles
around

Zappy intermission
Get the mustard, popcorn, cocaine
There's a gunboat on my navel
There are power lines in your hair

We're the plywood splinters
We're the All Edges Band
We cut you up and down
(cut and cut and cut and cut and cut
you up and down)

Hey come and hear our thumping
We're the All Edges Band
We can bring the dead around
make the stars hit the ground
bring the crocodiles
to town

Zappy intermission
Get the wall-eyes, earwigs, wrigglers
There are blue bones in the heaters
There are worms behind your iris

here they come!

dah- dah- dah-
oh mildewed booties

Listen to the tuba:
old stump feet
he got the ants up his rump
yeah! don't it hurt baby
(dooh- doohdah- dooh- doohdah)

just the other little ol' bitty night
those tweeky little stars dancing side to side
just walking to cool our brains from the traffic
we broke into this house and
killed everybody inside
(dooh- doohdah- dooh- doodah)
and graciously we ripped the walls
pencilled rude comments and all
(put your lightning rod in this hole you mother)
dah- dah- dah- dah-

Zappy intermission
Get the tweezers, needles, ice cubes
There's a dead boy in the light bulb
There's an eye inside my razor

We bring the crocodiles
to town!

them lazy palm oil trees.
ain't no pink elephant we got here
straight from Mother Escher
it's a blood chugging
man mucking, pond sucking
marsh- mellow eyed
turgid green
crocodile with this yellow guitar
stuck under his belt!

We're the All Edges Band
We knock the ceiling down
We snake and fake around
We're the All Edges Band
We'll even eat your lizard

We're the All Edges Band
We further cancer research
We're the All Edges Band
We start an organ Bank
We're the All Edges Band
We are really fussy eaters
We're the All-
We're the All-
We ain't got no round ends

Ruth Taylor

MARSH BASKETS

by day
she weaves
marsh baskets
    water gushing
       through and through
           her reeds

and the sweet rain
snags
in her grasses
    & rhymes

as storms do
in her marriages

       she weaves

marsh baskets
with secret washes
in her rushy songs
      and hours
of bloody thunder
     on her cheek
       to tame

by day
   she weaves
marsh baskets

loves you
with her other name.

Carole L. Ten Brink

EULOGY TO MY AFRICAN GOAT SKULL

Gone
in a fit of sanity
or spring cleaning.

My dry jewel
My porous stone
My own bone
    a hard and perfect shape of death
    a carved head
    a wind encaved

My ziz-zag, dry river seams
My chiseled holes where nerves went
My nothing manifesto

You live so real in my brain
Why can I never gaze again
at your petrified snow-scape
Never squeeze my crustacean sponge

In all the green jungle
In all the Mua Hills round Nairobi
Of all the elephant herds
Of all Ethiopia's bare genesis-rock
Of all the tongue-wooing song of women
    echoing from mountain to hut fire

You were the thing I loved

Not here
to oppose and vindicate my rose carpet
              my gold flowers
              my music of appalachian spring
              my sweaty excitement brewing.

AT FIVE O'CLOCK

At five o'clock
the sun takes walks with me
He holds his head high
Hot laughter, mouth foaming,
he pulls me up

At five o'clock he bounces
along row house roofs,
entertains me
He always keeps even with my step,
stops if I stop,
to taunt me
waiting for the next game

If I look at him squarely
he crawls outside himself
hanging there separate
with a fire sheath
lingering around him
Just like me slipping off a swimsuit
to feel the water everywhere

At five o'clock
the sun plays hide and seek
If I move sideways he disappears
When I move back he bounces out again
He's the dog and the ball
and he always wants to do it again

So - the sun and I rendez-vous
He's going east to west
I, north to south
The meeting is at five
It's pre-ordained and secret
and never can last very long

SOFT CIRCLES

A circle is a head with squiggles of hair around
if you wish, or a sun with spears as well
as a flower with petals and pistils
all have a multitude of orbs
more pleasant than the pustules of roseola
which are round as fish look
swimming in a pool reminds one
of concentric rings around pebbles plopping
which probably mirror centrifugal force
as when the sun throws streamers
outward would be analogous to the spider
spinning a web
or deductively
you get down to the way
a fly gets caught, bulls eye, or the eye itself
has a pupil and radiating lashes
which is something important to the whole idea
of a cell with a nucleus, or to the mushroom
with its stem, so that one could make more points
along this line, but prefers to go back to the center
which is, for instance, you can imagine a man running
tremendously, waving arms and legs
around the plump body trunk
a tree with branches and roots, diminutively speaking
a lady bug is similar from which one can induce
the whole rounded whale.

J.B. Thornton-McLeod

FLASH

....my father,   who has quietly gone out to take
                  the photograph of a thunderhead,

One day, that thunderhead will remove him,
           the sun will go on as before,
      that tireless blue machinery of the sky
                grind off in space.

        Flowers creak open,
              buds break out on the shores of my
                  window.

        But he won't come indoors

A FIRST TIME

Our relationship, shagged, brilliant ice-
beard of the Arctic: night's crenellated
dreams, beneath eyelids, half closed ecstasies,
ice melting between our legs,   trickles cold
exciting between my hands, love, cupping
your "sacrament" drink it down to its dregs:
collapsed, warmed mattress soaking with our
combined sweats; white sheets, rustle of words
articulate unspoken feelings,
only fingers & thighs talk: memory
sprouting ears all over my skin, soaks
up impressions, retinal shifts, sweet
oscillations: oiled Love's ball-bearings

a world over,   frees this amazing shudder.

Peter Van Toorn

MOUNTAIN GOING

With rips in my pockets big enough to
put my fists through, my coat in great shape too,
I made for the mountains, Muse, true to you.
Oh, la, la! the dreams of love I woke to.
Skies I wore for hats. So who walked by, hole
in his shorts, and stayed the night at Hotel
Big Bear to hear his stars swish and rustle?
Me, Tom Thumb, dreamer. Doodling my cuffs full,
leaning up against a ditch slope, left heel
under my bum, I'd smell some rose, feel
it stick to my brows like a sweat, and start
up singing some rhymes, keeping the beat light,
twanging the red elastic of my right
running shoe—its sole just jammed to my heart.

—from Rimbaud

MOUNTAIN RAIN

'If a sparrow comes before my window, I . . . pick
about the gravel.' - Keats

Rain, rain,
with your famous face,
walking down the back lane,
and looking over the roofs again!
Rain, rain,
coming down walls
in big wet balls,
washing cracks
in worms' backs,
and squabbling
with mud
in the drain!
Sweet, warm, birdfeatherruffling rain,

gluing lovers
to the ground,
throwing raindarts
into their hearts,
and walking
into telephone booths
and dialing
for more rain!
Vrishhh, preeeeng, roooooopah!
letting all the sound
out of tires,
trees, and cloud,
emptying a bladder
in the hall,
closing the red
fists of roses,
drying a storm
on the dome
of a thorn,
and hopping down
from thunder's brow!
Rain, rain, rain
landing
on cat's paws,
skipping around,
walking in tall
slanted boots
over boulevards
and roots,
and clapping
to make earth a mother again!

Rain, rain!

MOUNTAIN EASTER

There's silence, and there's silence. And then there's
a stillness to hold it all without noise.
Enough! The crazy fingers of the wind
just hit the roof and raise the red roof tiles
one Easter Sunday morning as the wind
walks and lies down and tries to get to sleep.
Getting up in a fed up restless rush,
he takes a jump into a leap and floats,
floats on all the floaters his body makes,
and floats and floats and floats, and bends in two,
twice, before floating by to a standstill,
breathing deep and breathing from his footsoles,
swinging his arms round in a lazy loop
as if swinging a pail full of fine snow,
not losing a flake as he throws himself
out into all corners of the city,
only to be back pressing his chest in
up against all sides of the house at once,
stretching them all, windows, walls, and roofsides,
stretching them, and shaking all the windows
for a moment, brushing glass on his sleeves,
bending them back into their places,
and all this time still pressing up against
the whole house on all sides so quietly
he hardly betrays his presence inside
any more than a fast midnight traffic
with its come and go surf, two streets over,
betrays the simmering sound of the sea—
a stillness to hold it all without noise,
the way corn hears the sun's booming hot voice
and holds it, and all in no more time than
it takes to ring a boy's bicycle bell.
The wind moves outside, blowing evenly
with all its belly, and sometimes blowing
on his fingers hard enough to blow out
the candle in the moon that keeps his nails
hard and cardsharp, clear for his mind to glow,
while fingering the cracks by the window,
all the cracks between putty, glass and wood,
fingering the knifecut under the door,

fingering the wrinkle of the keyhole,
and fingering for places to put snow,
hollows to splash full with one crystal blow.
　　His knees are turtle backs, pads to roll on,
stay still on, or bend a whole wall back on,
as if bending back and stringing a bow.
　　And his shoulders, that are sometimes covered
by the longest black hair, he can roll back
as if to let a yoke down, or roll back
to harden into a long shoulder pole
and hang twice his own weight from at ends, so
with both arms out, and his hair combed out wide,
he's feathered all along his shoulder blade
on which to move many times his own weight,
and move it forward now, as if on wheels.
　　But to come back to the wind and his ways.
A woman walks naked inside the house,
and is not seen. It is not only dark
but the street lights will only just show through
all the many fast driving flakes of snow
driving past the windows out of the dark
on the wind when he's all flakes in the dark,
when he's a falling of flakes in the air
and he shakes the poplars and the phone poles,
shakes them, pole by pole, and not from the hips,
nor from the knees, but from the top branches
down to the roots where he rolls out on them,
under the ground, where he rolls on the balls
of his feet, into the ball of the earth.
　　Go through him when he rushes round the house
and pours in at the windows like a cat
pushing all the air out of the house,
bales of air, ropes of air, and rooms of air,
pulling with his back out, pulling air in,
pushing with his back in, pushing air out,
all without brushing a flake of snow off.
　　Though the wind's mad to get into the house,
the wind's just as mad to get out again,
and will not stand for the closing of doors,
but going bareheaded, he moves freely,
and sometimes carries a damp that not all
the towels on the clothes line can dry off.

One Easter Sunday the wind does not rise
blue in the face as Christ, the rising Jew,
but as man of wind, wood, mountain, and dew.
    He's not here or there, this or that, just wind
lying down on the air only the birds
know how to sail on. There's a coat of dew
on the windshields, on the grass, and on you.

MOUNTAIN STORM

*'The bitter and the sweet come fom outside, the hard
from within.' - Einstein*

Maybe a walk out in this kind of weather
can straighten you out,
even grow on you,
but you have other things to listen to.
So when the growling out there
swings your door open
and knocks a pan off the stove,
unless elves skip in to mop up for you,
or the fire smeared over the floor is of bronze,
forget it.
It's another kind of weather
makes you feel
up to it—
taking a walk,
opening your coat at the throat,
stretching out,
chewing on a milky nib of grass,
dialing the clouds with your big toe.
And even though an out and out storm out there,
breathing down your neck
and skimming the fat from your hair,
can make you feel like spitting your teeth out
as far as some stars,
and do it,
easily,
true,
as a chainsaw rips a century of rock maple in two,

it's no weather
to open a moody maple like an old book,
finger its fresh Indian feathers,
talk a tune out of it,
or take it for a pencil behind an ear of the moon.
So if some rage
(coming over you out of the blue)
makes you feel like bending your head down,
ducking out inside the heart side of your coat,
deep as the storm's strong,
and plucking a flame from a match
to get a glow going—
incense, tobacco, candlewax: stick, bowl or wick—
don't let it eat your heart out
or throw you off.
It's another kind of weather altogether
bobs the world back up under the balls of your feet,
with some of the planets
and nearly all of the spheres—
juicy pinks, reds, golds, blacks, browns, ivories, and blues—
singing
to your ears,
in, or out of, the weather
still banging into the mountains to tune the trees.

MOUNTAIN FRIENDS

So what am I—stuffed cabbage?—that you come here
with Buddy every night? What are you doing,
standing by the door whistling a tune, fooling
with the snow? Okay, so I was a goner,
a guy to roll your eyeballs at—let him stare
at the whites of your eyes rolling with feeling.
(I should ride a pickle over the ceiling,
no?) How many times did you say, 'Oyez, Peter,
as long as you're here and your doorbell's kaput,
why don't you get yourself a dog, who'll tell you,
with a bark like Buddy's, deep as a sawcut,
that Leopold Plotek, the Polish painter,
is waiting, book in hand, outside your front door—
your friend, you jerk!—on his way home from Kung Fu?'

Jeremy Walker

VISIONARY ELEGY

    :Apple-sweet
the beer goes down my throat:
it's a hot & humid night,
& tonight I am too tired to resist
& fight: even this cigarette tastes like nut,
crunchy, chocolaty,
    as if my childhood was coming back to me in fruit:
That's how I thought
last night, late on, as I
sat drinking beer, alone and lonely,
in the Swiss Hut: all around me
sat in their twos & threes
the young French, English, & American,
& up at the bar a lonely and angry veteran
fought with his neighbours:
'No respect', he said,
resentfully & only one agreed,
sitting beside him on his left-hand side:
And I thought:
               Age?
    surely better wisdom—what would Socrates
    have said? That man there,
    for example: to be pitied,
    sure: without condescension: but honoured,
    no. How narrow he has made
    himself: or been made. Length of years
    makes no man or woman wise:
    let us respect the young, then, if they be wise,
      above their elders.
A blonde girl, sitting back of me,
wearing a purple band around her forehead,
caught my eye there three or four nights running:
our eyes kept catching again tonight
over my left and twisting shoulder,
& I dreamt. I thought:

My life has been a horror,
to speak plainly:
a mountainous and arid desert
thru which I go, weeping
inwardly, fists clenched tight:
now, reaching thirty-three,
a no-man's land between youth and age,
I sit remembering Hart Crane,
& others, Herbert, Hölderin,
Leopardi; men I feel to be my brothers:
& others greater, Baudelaire,
and Blake, poets to whom I do not dare
compare myself: what I remember
principally tonight is that they were unhappy men,
who died crazy, drunk, or sick,
suicides & self-tormentors,
brimming with fear, remorse, a sense of loss:
(Over sandy wastes
went Psyche,
towards the death-filled scorpion-filled hills,
rising like tumuli before the sinking sun,
weeping: steadfast,
however, she got her precious water
& won back Love's love,
& beauty too: faithful soul,
to her God bride she came thru suffering,
who as a young bride, too early
dared to lift her candle to his face,
seeing in the mid-night what had been forbidden her:
a wind rose, & howling, swept away
fragments of her life, her palace, & her God.)
    :Bitter & deep men,
    they walked thru their lives
    as if carrying some great secret:
    coming in the end to 'despondency and madness',
    as one wrote, they left the world
    scattered with bright flashes
    from a world they dreamed—
    or remembered, from their childhood
    'clouds of glory': innocents,

they cursed, whored, broke homes,
played ducks & drakes with their friends' money,
became fierce, stiff, proud, obsessed self-haters.
I too am like them, God help me:
success I have had, marriage, & children:
but if one should ask me, Who are you?,
I should say: by profession philosopher,
but poet, by vocation.
My life wd be a naming of the names
of all the girls & boys that I have loved:
this truth wd be a clear and killing cure.
A lonely child,
a lonely adolescence,
I still dream of the sea where I was born,
an amniotic fluid
into which I plunge each night,
& drown myself in its green withdrawals.
I have fled, & turned,
& always the whirling wind has found me.
Sere, my fall comes early: the short day closes down.
    :Lowell, your Bostonian cadences,
    more harsh and sweet than any metaphysical's, seduce us
    like the crash of breakers on the distant beach:
    pain, poured out in truth
    on these small pages,
    becomes a sobering wine
    for us who read:
    say, for us who do not know you,
    can his friends save a man?
    —It was never so, friend.—
Two lights swung to & fro
in the wind, near the door:
as I pensively fingered my glass,
turning it round and round,
I saw my life, as in a vision,
clear & remote, as thru an inverted glass,
astronomers of the present,
we see our toys, pictured & orderly.
Often at the end the wise
bow before what's beautiful.
& Poets, too, seeing
too young a fruit they cannot seize,

become at first confused,
& try to snatch the hanging branch;
failing, live on in thirst for that water,
& come in the end to be
water-bearers, gift-bringers
themselves for others, whom unknowingly
the wise honour after their death,
& who go down, mostly, to a bitter & early grave.

addy Webb

HUMMING BIRDS

it was very sudden

buds were slowly turning back
their petals when the birds descended
   out of the sun
darted in straight swift jabs
and oblique angles
                     then stopped
treading air   beaks extended
                 their snaky throats pulsating
                 their wings a blur of light

two aerial motor-bicycles
that hummed and buzzed and jazzed

they sucked
           like small refuelling
space-craft coupled to parent ships
then backed away
              hovered
then sipped some more

                  (they can go off
in any direction   like exploding
fire-crackers on quick rays of flight
in vertical or reverse take-off
and they can put out their brights
dimming to dull olive-dun jade
or leap again to life
then vanish)

                    two pairs of jewel thieves
ruby and emerald
                          dive-bombed
    my fuschias
                    and
                          after the attack
the only sign   a slight wobble
    of purple and red flowers

      as if a wearer of ear-drops
          shook her head

CHERRY PICKING

shaken from sleep
                    I stumble
clumsy as a camel
                    my dream-dried
eyelids heavy and thick
my right hand a numb balled fist
and stagger to the window

      they are at it again

      in the orchard below
      a relentless machine
      metronomes down the rows
      in a massacre of cherries

      they come spilling down
      drumming a red tattoo
      on the tight stretched cloth
      and rolling   rolling
      like so many bloody heads

is it foolish of me to think
they submit too easily?
such progress tells off my years
it is part of nature's treachery
unnecessarily hurried

so short a time it seems
                    since

I was counting their pithy pits
to tell my fortune by

    my eyes play tricks

    see a small lithe boy
    wearing earrings of cherries
    spitting stones from
    a cherry-tongued cheek

    tumble from a branch

lie still
      at the tree's foot

SIDLESHAM HARBOR

this low tide the mud flats lie
smooth and shiny like grey seals
basking on dark green cloths of
purslane   with rattles of seeds

the surface is broken by
popping and gurgling ripples
which suck and sigh as they dry
while the waders and dippers
leave three-fingered footprints one's
eye can distinguish between
by the pattern
            much small fry
is stranded   gasping   to die
soon
      and in marjoram's late-
flowering bloom thickly are seen
long-winded beetles the night's frost
will kill

      the harbor's black-edged
today - an envelope
of condolence - bordered by
many small skeletons -
            lost

gulls   never to dance or slope
down the wind
                    a drowned rat
a large dog on its side
and more than a million crabs

back on shore   where the spent
sea-rocket has fired its last
lilac cluster of stars
                    bats
dive and skim
                    while   on the flats
    the sun's death crimsons a mast

Jerry Wexler

SO THIS IS WHAT IT'S LIKE TO BE IN MONTREAL IN THE MIDDLE OF A COLD JANUARY

I met Jonathan at the Cafe Santropol near the mountain. It was January 17 and it was freezing outside. Jonathan looked his haggard self. He was lean and had a thin drawn-in face, and always had a lanky posture. He was wearing a red sweatshirt and a yellow tuque. No coat. On his feet he had torn red adidas. He lived in a storefront just across the street from the cafe so I imagine he had not come very far and that was why he was dressed so thinly. He joined me for a coffee. I was sad because I had split up with my girlfriend. His girlfriend had left him three months before. We sat for awhile reading the Gazette, drinking coffee and eating strudel. I mentioned that I was listless and he invited me over to his home, the old Liberty Cheese storefront that he lived in.

We sat in his makeshift kitchen. His furnace had broken, his house was freezing. We sat by his stove, the only source of warmth, scarves around our necks, tuques on our heads, feet in the oven. I was smoking cigarettes. I never really smoked before, but now it seemed like an appropriate thing to do. Jonathan put on his Grateful Dead album. They were singing about hitch-hiking in the American Southwest and I told Jonathan about a trip I had done the previous winter to Arizona. There I had found a reinhabited copper mining town called Bisbee that rested on the slopes of a mountain. From a distance it looked like a town out of the old west. The town was inhabited by young people like us and it had a good feeling to it. Jonathan told me I should stop moping about my girlfriend. He was five years younger than me but I suppose he was wise.

So there we were, feet in the oven, scarves around our necks, freezing our butts, talking about lost women and far off towns, and it occurred to me that this is what it's like to be in Montreal in the middle of a cold January.

Shulamis Yelin

PASSAGE

My days, once
    meteor-lit and conjuring the heavens,
lie waste now under neon-lighted
    glare.
Dehydrated, smartly packaged,
    rightly priced,
displayed to vantage in supermart
    of social contact,
they wait for homebound marketers
returning from the fair,
from bargaining and testing,
to toss them in their carriage basket
    of desire
for easy quick consumption.

CONDITIONING

What could I know of horses
when the only ones I recalled
were the mare that pulled the milk wagon,
or the fruit-man's filly,
or that poor nag,
blanketed with wretched patchwork,
stopped shame-faced before our door
and door of neighbours,
while aproned housewives from cold flats
came to pick and choose the largest
    sawdust-covered block
on which to seat their meat and milk
for comfortable freshness;
or that Belgian stud, rich-muscled,
heavy-penised,
which advertised the Beer of Men.

What could I know other than
that a horse could draw a load,
was patient for an apple or a carrot
or a pat between the blinkers,
weathering all seasons
and enriching newly-fallen snow
with hot and gleaming sparrow-fare;
or the unreal image
of that powerful and potent satisfier
        of a shameful thirst . . .

Noah Zacharin

SOON TO BE TITLED

Pleased with the seed her man has given
her insides have taken one favored from the river
and it has planted like a flag of declaration
into new unbruised land. And from this
meager beginning begins the increase of cells
to shape form & face, a mix of the two
whose fusion led to fusion that leads
to fission & the yeast-rise of her belly.
Winter-white it moves like spring earth.

Inside a blessing grows.
Watch and see the evidence spread
silk as dawnlake rippling.
Lean your ear against the smooth,
close enough you hear sea-sound, moon-work
from where the river ran to, tide beats;
where you imagine the blind wet source
curled like a conch, preparing to unroll
like a horn-heralded proclamation.

Biographical Notes

Mona Elaine Adilman
A Montrealer and McGill graduate. She has taught ecology and literature at Concordia University. Her free-lance articles on environmental and political issues have been widely published.
Recent books: *Piece Work*, Borealis Press (1979); *Cult of Concrete*, Bonsecours Editions (1979).

Robert Allen
Born in Bristol, England in 1946. Has lived in a variety of places in North America, including Toronto, Ohio, New York and Prince Edward Island. Now lives in Ayer's Cliff, Quebec. He is an associate editor of *Matrix* and one of the founding editors of *The Moosehead Review*.
Recent books: *The Hawryliw Process*, The Porcupine's Quill (1980, 1981); *The Assumption of Private Lives*, New Delta (1977)

John Asfour
Born February 10, 1945 in Aiteneat, Lebanon. Moved to Canada in 1968. Teaches at Dawson College in Montreal and is completing a doctorate at McGill University.
Recent books: *Land of Flowers and Guns*, DC Books (1981); *Nisan*, Fiddlehead Poetry Books (1976).

Brian Bartlett
Has been a Montrealer since 1975, after having spent his youth in New Brunswick, which he still visits every year. Also a writer of fiction, Bartlett has published stories in *78: Best Canadian Stories* (Oberon) and *Aurora: New Canadian Writing 1980 (Doubleday)*. At present he is completing *Fearful Children*, a long novel he has been working on for three years.
Recent books: *Cattail Week*, Villeneuve (1981).

Henry Beissel
A widely published poet, playwright, translator and editor. He was born in 1929 in Cologne, Germany and came to Canada in 1951. Teaches at Concordia University in Montreal.
Recent books: *Cantos North*, Penumbra Press (1982), *Under Coyote's Eye*, Quadrant Editions (1980, 1981).

Guy Birchard
Born in 1949 in Portage-la-Prairie. Birchard has been published in several literary magazines.

Recent books: *Baby Grand,* Brick/Nairn (1979).

Steven Brockwell
Born in St-Louis de Terrebonne, Quebec in 1963. He is attending McGill University.
Recent books: *Lakeshore Poets,* Muses' Company (1981)

Leonard Cohen
Leonard Norman Cohen was born in Montreal and educated at McGill University. He dropped out of graduate school at Columbia University to write and to perform music in Montreal nightclubs. Now internationally known as a songwriter and entertainer, Cohen continues to publish books of poetry and prose.
Recent books: *Death of a Lady's Man,* McClelland and Stewart (1978).

Antonio D'Alfonso
Born August 5, 1953 in Montreal. Graduated from Loyola College and the Université de Montréal with an M.A. in Science and Semiology. He is a poet, critic, filmmaker and founder of Guernica Editions.
Recent books: *Queror,* Guernica Editions (1979)

Frances Davis
Born in Winnipeg, Manitoba in 1936 and graduated with a B.A. (Hon. Eng.) from the University of Manitoba in 1958. Master's Degree in English from University of Toronto in 1961. Presently teaches writing and literature at Vanier College.

Jane Dick
After living in Montreal for several years now resides in Winnipeg.
Recent books: *Conceptions,* Guernica Editions (1980)

Louis Dudek
Born February 6, 1918 in Montreal. He completed a B.A. at McGill University and a M.A. and Ph.D. at Columbia University. He has taught modern poetry, Canadian literature and European literature at McGill University for the past thirty years.
Recent books: *Continuation I,* Véhicule Press (1981); *Cross-Section: Poems 1940-1980,* Coach House Press (1980); *Selected Essays and Criticism,* Tecumseh Press (1978).

Béla Egyedi
Born in Hungary (1913); MA (PhD-cand) Budapest: linguistics/literature, modern languages. During siege of Budapest, collared by the incoming Russians: forced-labour camp; work-accident; escaped from military hospital. 1948 fled country altogether. Paris sojourn, then to Canada (since '51). Canadian citizen. Recent books: *mushi-no-koe,* Swamp Press (1979).

R.G. Everson
Born in Oshawa in 1903. Lives in Montreal.
Recent books: *Carnival,* Oberon; *Indian Summer,* Oberon.

Patricia Renée Ewing
Born in Montréal. Spent 2½ years in Spain where she wrote her first book of poems.
Recent books: *The Other Land,* Bonsecours Editions (1974).

Endre Farkas
Born March 11, 1948 in Hungary. Moved to Canada in 1956. Teaches at John Abbott College. Founder of The Muses' Company.
Recent books: *From Here to Here,* The Muses' Company (1982); *Face-Off,* The Muses' Company (1980); *Romantic at Heart and Other Faults,* Cross-Country Press (1979).

Raymond Filip
"I make my living as a musician and writer." Runs the multicultural reading series *Pluriel.*
Recent books: *Somebody Told Me I Look Like Everyman,* Pulp Press (1978).

Marco Fraticelli
Lives in Montreal and is the editor of *The Alchemist.*
Recent books: *Instants,* Guernica Editions (1979).

Bill Furey
Bill Furey was born in Newfoundland and moved to Montreal in 1968. His poetry has appeared in several Canadian magazines.
Recent books: *Night Letters,* Signal Editions (1982).

Gary Geddes
Gary Geddes has taught widely in universities across Canada. In addition to writing regular articles and reviews, he is general editor of Studies in Canadian Literature (Douglas and McIntyre) and has edited four anthologies: *20th-Century Poetry & Poetics, 15 Canadian Poets Plus 5, Skookum Wawa: Writings of the Canadian Northwest,* and *Divided We Stand.* He teaches English and Creative Writing at Concordia University and runs the press Quadrant Editions.
Recent books: *The Acid Test,* Turnstone Press (1981); *War & other measures,* Talonbooks (1976).

John Glassco
Born 1909 in Montreal and educated at McGill University. Spent the last years of his life living in Foster, Quebec.
Principal publications: *Poems of Saint-Denys-Garneau,* Oberon (1975); *Selected Poems,* Oxford University Press (1971); *Memoirs of Montparnasse* (1970).

Artie Gold
"born January 16, 1947 Brockville, Ontario. Raised in Montreal. University, Colorado School of Mines from which I dropped out after an extended year. Began serious writing in 1968, activity mostly directed inside poetry. "
Recent books: *before Romantic Words,* Véhicule Press (1979); *Some of the Cat Poems,* CrossCountry Press (1978).

Raymond Gordy
A native Quebecker, born on October 25, 1940. A graduate of Loyola College and McGill University. Practising lawyer.
Recent books: *Doing Time,* Poverty Press (1974).

Ralph Gustafson
Ralph Gustafson is a kind of Renaissance Man of Quebec's Eastern Townships where he was born and educated. He has received degrees from Bishop's University, Oxford University and is Honourary D. Litt from Mount Allison, and Honourary D.C.L. from Bishop's.
He has written over a dozen volumes of poetry and received the Governor General's Award for Poetry in 1974. His influential anthologies of Canadian writing, including the *Penguin Book of Canadian Verse,* and his many broadcasts on music for the CBC, have made him widely known as an editor and critic.
Recent books: *At the Oceans's Verge,* Black Swan Books (1982); *Gradations of Grandeur,* Sono Nis Press (1982); *Conflicts of Spring,* McClelland and Stewart (1981).

Jack Hannan
Born in Montreal, January 14, 1949. Co-Editor of the M.B.M. Monograph Series, published by Mansfield Book Mart, that appeared in the late 1970's and early eighties.
Recent books: *For the Coming Surface,* Dreadnaught Press (1980); *Points North of A,* Villeneuve Publications (1980); *Peeling Oranges in the Shade,* Paget Press (1978).

Michael Harris
Born in Glasgow, Scotland in 1944. Teaches at Dawson College. He edits Signal Editions for Vehicle Press.
Recent books: *Grace,* New Delta (1977); *Sparks,* New Delta (1976).

Neil Henden
Born in Montreal in 1960. Lived on and around the West Island. Jobs have included: coat checker, maintenance, summer camp counsellor, bookstore clerk. Presently enrolled in the McGill faculty of education and works as an educator with retarded children.
Recent books: *Lakeshore Poets,* The Muses' Company (1981).

Laurence Hutchman
Born July 4, 1948 in Belfast, Northern Ireland. Presently teaching at the University of Alberta in Edmonton.
Recent books: *Explorations,* DC Books (1975).

D.G. Jones
Born in Bancroft, Ontario, in 1929. Studied at McGill and Queen's Universities. Lives in North Hatley, Quebec, and teaches in the Département les études anglaises, l'Université de Sherbrooke.
Recent books: *Under the Thunder the Flowers Light Up the Earth,* Coach House Press (1977).

Jim Joyce
Born 1947. Teaches Human Philosophy at John Abbott College. His poems have been published in several Canadian journals.

Janet Kask
Born December 18, 1937 in Seattle, Washington (Dual U.S.-Canadian citizenship until 1960, then became full Canadian citizen. Has worked for the last twenty years as a journalist, broadcaster and commentator. Teaches journalism at Concordia University.

Tom Konyves
Born July 13, 1947 in Budapest, Hungary. Escaped during the Hungarian Revolution of 1956. Educated and re-educated. Married, divorced. 1 son, Michael (The Great). Taught literature for a few years, worked in publishing, public relations, pop bottles. Became a member of Véhicule Art, 1978. Put "Poetry On The Buses." Multi-media oriented, his recent works are "poetry performances."
Recent books: *Poetry in Performance,* The Muses' Company (1982); *No Parking,* Véhicule Press (1978).

Rochl Korn
Born in Poland in 1898. Well-published in Yiddish, and in translation, in North America and Europe. The author continues to write and receive visitors from her home in Montreal. The two poems included in this anthology were originally published in Russia in 1928.
Recent books: *Canadian Yiddish Writing,* Harvest House (1976) and *The Poets of Canada,* Hurtig (1978)

Helen Kosacky
Born in Montreal in 1956. Started writing stories at the age of eight and poetry at fourteen. B.A. in English Literature from McGill, 1979. Currently writing a book of poems based on Tarot cards.

Greg Lamontagne
Born in Petrolia, Ontario in 1962. Currently a student at John Abbott College.
Recent books: *Lakeshore Poets,* The Muses' Company (1981)

Claudia Lapp
Born Aug. 7, 1946 in Stuttgart, Germany. B.A. from Bennington College.
Moved to Montreal in 1968. Worked at the Montreal Museum of Fine Arts,
then taught at John Abbott College 1972-79. Organized the pilot reading
series at Véhicule. Presently living in Columbia, Maryland.
Recent books: *Honey,* Véhicule Press (1977)

Irving Layton
Born 1912 in Rumania; educated at McGill University; associated with Dudek
and Souster in founding Contact Press. Nominated in 1981 for the Nobel
Prize for Literature.
Recent books: *A Wild Peculiar Joy,* McClelland and Stewart (1982) *Droppings from Heaven,* McClelland and Stewart (1981); *The Love Poems of Irving Layton,* McClelland and Stewart (1980); *For My Neighbours in Hell,* Mosaic Press/Valley Editions (1980).

Ross Leckie
Ross Leckie was born in Lachine, Quebec in 1953. For two years he was
editor of the monthly magazine *Montreal Writers' Forum.*
Recent books: *The Sound In A Forest,* Signal Editions (1982).

Carole H. Leckner
Born in Montreal, January 13, 1946. Travelled in Europe and Israel, 1967-69.
Writes in several genres: poetry, fiction, and film. Has worked as a publisher,
editor, book reviewer and journalist. M.A. in Creative Writing from Concordia University in 1979.
Recent books: *Seasons In Transition,* Fiddlehead Poetry Books (1979).

Seymour Levitan
Has recently edited and translated a collection of Rochl Korn's poetry. His
translations have been included in *The Spice Box, Poets Out of Canada,* and
Ashes Out of Dust. He lives in Vancouver.

Stephen Luxton
Stephen Luxton was born in England in 1946 and has lived there and in the
United States as well as Canada. He moved into the Montreal area in 1976 and
has kept body and soul together by teaching at Champlain College, Concordia
University and Vanier College. For Luxton, Poetry provides a parachute to
ease The Fall...
Recent books: *Late Romantics,* Moosehead Press (1980).

Keitha MacIntosh

Sixth generation québecoise. Scot-Irish ancestry. Mother tongue: Gaelic. Born in Lachine, Quebec. M.A., Creative Writing, Concordia University, 1977. Teaches at Vanier College.

Recent books: *Chateauguay Poems,* South Western Ontario Poetry Press (1982); *The Crow Sits High in the Lilac Tree,* Kateri Press (1982).

Avrum Malus

Born in Montreal in 1938. Went to school at McGill, Rutgers, and Université de Montréal. Now teaches at Université de Sherbrooke. Lives near the village of Massawippi in the Eastern Townships.

Recent books: *I Set the Fire Which Destroyed Our Home,* Paget Press (1978).

John McAuley

Born in 1947. Lives in Montreal. Edited *Maker* from 1976-79. Graduated from Concordia University where he now teaches. Ran the Véhicule poetry series with Bob Galvin and Stephen Morrissey in 1976-77.

Recent books: *What Henry Hudson Found,* Véhicule Press (1979); *Hazardous Renaissance,* CrossCountry Press (1978); *Mattress Testing,* Cross Country Press (1978).

Robert McGee

Born in Otter Lake, Quebec in 1952 of Irish and French-Canadian parents. Lives in Montreal. Recent books: *The Shanty Horses,* New Delta (1977).

Anne McLean

Born in Montreal. Recent books: *Lil,* New Delta (1977).

Mary Melfi

Born in Italy, 1951. Graduated from Loyola College and obtained a Masters in Library Science from McGill University. Writes poetry, short stories, plays and novels.

Recent books: *A Queen Is Holding a Mummified Cat,* Guernica Editions (1982).

Stephen Morrissey

Stephen Morrissey was born in Montreal on April 27, 1950. He completed a B.A. at Sir George Williams University and an M.A. at McGill University. With wife Pat Walsh and son Jake he lives outside of Huntingdon, fifty miles south-west of Montreal. He teaches at Champlain College.

Recent books: *Divisions,* Coach House Press (1982); *The Trees of Unknowing,* Véhicule Press (1978).

Henry Moscovitch

Henry Moscovitch is a Montreal poet. He was educated at McGill University and at Columbia University. He is the author of two books of poetry that

appeared in the 1950's: *The Serpent Ink* and *The Laughing Storm.*
Recent books: *New Poems,* Mosaic Press/Valley Editions (1982).

Sharon H. Nelson
Sharon H. Nelson is a Montreal writer and is managing editor of Metonymy Productions. She has been a founding coordinator of the Poets at Powerhouse readings and of the Feminist Caucus of the League of Canadian Poets.
Recent books: *blood poems,* Fiddlehead Poetry Books (1979).

Ken Norris
Born in New York City, April 3, 1951. Currently working for the C.I.A. in the Southern Hemisphere.
Recent books: *Eight Odes,* The Muses' Company (1982); *To Sleep, To Love,* Guernica Editions (1982); *Autokinesis,* CrossCountry Press (1980); *The Book of Fall,* Maker Press (1979).

Rena Okada
Born in Salt Lake City, Utah and works in Montreal. She is currently working on a novel and is a member of a small, informal group of writers who meet irregularly, drink tea and read their works-in-progress to each other amidst laughter and criticism.

Marc Plourde
Marc Plourde was born in Montreal in 1951 of French and English Canadian parents. He has published two books of poetry, a book of short stories and eight or nine volumes of translations.
Recent books: *The Alchemy of the Body* (Poems of Juan Garcia), Guernica Editions (1982); *The Spark Plug Thief,* New Delta (1977).

Martin Reyto
Martin Reyto was born in Budapest in 1948, has lived in Canada since 1956, and in Montreal since 1979.
Recent books: *The Cloned Mammoth,* Quadrant Editions (1981).

Filippo Salvatore
Filippo Salvatore was born in Guglionesi, Italy on January 27, 1948. He came to Canada in 1964. He graduated from McGill University and has a Ph.D. from Harvard. In addition to teaching humanities at Champlain College, Salvatore is sessional lecturer of contemporary Italian literature and cinema at the Université de Montréal.
Recent books: *Suns of Darkness.* Guernica Editions (1980).

Robyn Sarah
Born in New York, 1949. Grew up in Montreal. Studied at McGill University and at the Quebec Conservatoire of Music. In 1976 co-founded (with husband

Fred Louder) Villeneuve, a Montreal small press operating out of home. Teaches at Champlain Regional College. Two children.
Recent books: *The Space Between Sleep and Waking,* Villeneuve (1981); *Shadowplay,* Fiddlehead Poetry Books (1978).

Lazar Sarna
Born December 9, 1948. Practices law in Montreal. He is currently working on a novel. Recent books: *Letters of State,* Porcupine's Quill (1978).

F.R. Scott
F.R. Scott was born and brought up in Quebec City, and educated at Bishop's, Oxford and McGill. He taught school, practised law, and then joined the McGill Law Faculty as full-time teacher and later Dean. In 1925 he joined with A.J.M. Smith in founding the *McGill Fortnightly Review,* and was an editor of the *Canadian Mercury, Preview* and *Northern Review.*
Recent Books: *The Collected Poems of F.R. Scott,* McClelland and Stewart (1981); *Poems of French Canada,* Blackfish Press (1978); *Essays on The Constitution: Aspects of Canadian Law and Politics* (1978)

Daniel Sloate
Daniel Sloate was born in Ontario. At the University of Western Ontario he became interested in theatre and participated in the Shakespeare Festival at Stratford. He is an associate professor in the Linguistics Department at the Université de Montréal.
Recent books: *Dead Shadows,* Guernica Editions (1982); *A Taste Of Earth, A Taste Of Flame,* Guernica Editions (1981).

David Solway
8. 12. 41: Mtl. Teaches at John Abbott College.
Recent books: *Selected Poems,* Signal Editions (1981); *The Mulberry Men,* Signal Editions (1981); *Mephistopheles and the Astronaut,* Mosaic Press/ Valley Editions (1979).

Richard Sommer
Richard Sommer was born and raised in Minnesota. He has lived, taught, written poetry in Montreal for the past twenty-one years.
Recent books: *The Other Side of Games,* New Delta (1977); *Milarepa,* New Delta (1976); *Left Hand Mind,* New Delta (1976).

Ben Soo
Born in Hong Kong in 1960. Educated at St. Thomas High School, Pointe Claire, Quebec and at John Abbott College.
Recent books: *Lakeshore Poets,* Muses' Company (1981)

Ruth Taylor
Born on Ile Perrot, 1961. Editor of *Locus* at John Abbott College in 1979 and

co-organizer of the Véhicule Poetry Reading Series in 1980.

Carole L. Ten Brink
Born 1940 in Holland, Michigan. Has an M.A. from McGill.
Recent books: *Thaw & Fire*, Bonsecours Editions (1978).

Joan B. Thornton-McLeod
Born in Montreal, 1944. Family in Quebec for 300 years. Studied six years at Montreal Museum of Fine Arts.
Recent books: *La Corriveau & The Blond & Other Poems*, Bonsecours Editions (1975).

Peter Van Toorn
Born in 1944, in a bunker near the Hague. *In Guildenstern County* was published in 1973, *Leeway Grass* in 1970. Teacher at John Abbott College.

Jeremy Walker
Born in England in 1936. Associate Professor of Philosophy at McGill University since 1966. Married and divorced, two children.
Recent books: *Apocalypse With Figures*, DC Books (1974).

Paddy Webb
Paddy Webb was born in Essex, England. She came to Canada in 1966, where she teaches at McGill University. She has been writing and publishing poems since 1963.
Recent books: *Children & Milkweed*, Priapus Press (1978).

Jerry Wexler
Born in Montreal in 1950. Taught English and Cinema in CEGEPs for five years. Currently working full time as a short story writer and dramatic scriptwriter for the N.F.B., C.B.C., and the private film industry.

Shulamis Yelin
Born in Montreal. Educated at the Université de Montréal, post-graduate studies at Columbia. Won the LaMed Award for her monograph on Carol Ryan in 1961. Presently involved in Jewish and Comparative Literature.
Recent books: *Canadian Jewish Anthology* (1981)

Noah Zacharin
Born in Montreal in 1957. In final year of dentistry at McGill University. Also a guitarist, singer and songwriter, he is currently recording an album of original music.

Acknowledgements

The editors are grateful to the poets themselves for permission to publish their copyrighted poems. Many of the poems in this anthology were first published in literary magazines; some have appeared in books by individual poets. Grateful acknowledgement is made to the following:

For Mona Adilman to Borealis Press and the author; for Robert Allen to New Delta, *The Cincinnati Poetry Review* and the author; for John Asfour to DC Books and the author; for Brian Bartlett to *Queen's Quarterly, The Fiddle-head*, Villeneuve Publications and the author; for Henry Beissel to DC Books and the author; for Guy Birchard to Brick/Nairn and the author; for Leonard Cohen to McClelland and Stewart, The Canadian Publishers, and the author; for Antonio D'Alfonso to Guernica Editions and the author; for Frances Davis to *Quarry, Canadian Women Studies* and the author; for Jane Dick to Guernica Editions and the author; for Louis Dudek to *CVII*, Coach House Press and the author; for Béla Egyedi to Swamp Press and the author; for R.G. Everson to Oberon Press and the author; for Patricia Renee Ewing to *Mundus Artium, Montreal Poems* and the author; for Endre Farkas to *Prism International, Mouse Eggs, Writ*, CrossCountry Press and the author; for Raymond Filip to *Northern Journey, Versus, Gut*, Pulp Press and the author; for Marco Frati-celli to Guernica Editions and the author; for Bill Furey to Véhicule Press and the author; for Gary Geddes to Turnstone Press and the author; for John Glassco to Oberon Press and the author; for Artie Gold to *Stooge, Versus, Bezoar*, Talonbooks, CrossCountry Press, Maker Press, Vehicule Press and the author; for Raymond Gordy to Poverty Press and the author; for Ralph Gustafson to McClelland and Stewart, The Canadian Publishers, *Cross-Country* and the author; for Jack Hannan to Villeneuve Publications, *Atropos, Montreal Writers' Forum*, Dreadnaught Press and the author; for Neil Henden to *Locus*, The Muses' Company and the author; for Michael Harris to *The Atlantic Monthly*, New Delta and the author; for Laurence Hutchman to *Versus, Prism International* and the author; for D.G. Jones to Coach House Press and the author; for Jim Joyce to the author; for Janet Kask to *The Fiddlehead* and the author; for Rochl Korn to Harvest House, to translator Seymour Levitan and the author; for Helen Kosacky to the author: for Greg Lamontagne to the author; for Claudia Lapp to Maker Press and the author; for Irving Layton to McClelland and Stewart, The Canadian Publishers, Valley/Mosaic Press and the author; for Ross Leckie to *Montreal Writers' Forum* and the author; for Carole H. Leckner to Fiddlehead Books and the author; for Stephen Luxton to *Matrix,* Moosehead Press and the author; for Avrum Malus to Paget Press and the author; for Keitha MacIntosh to *Poetry Toronto Newsletter* and the author; for John McAuley to CrossCountry Press, Véhicule Press and the author; for Robert McGee to CVII, New Delta and the author; for Anne McLean to the author; for Mary Melfi to *Matrix,* Guernica Editions and the author; for Stephen Morrissey to *The Antigonish Review, Mouse Eggs,* Vehicule Press and the author; for Henry Moscovitch to Mosaic Press/Valley Editions and the author; for Sharon H. Nelson to *Stuffed Crocodile,* Fiddlehead Poetry Books and the author; for Ken Norris to *Anthol, The Antigonish Review,* Véhicule Press, CrossCountry Press, The Muses' Company and the author; for Rena Okada to *Process* and the author; for Marc Plourde to *The Antigonish Review, Tamarack Review,* Torchy Wharf and the author; for Martin Reyto to Quadrant Editions and the author; for Filippo Salvatore to Guernica Editions and the author; for Robyn Sarah to *The Antigonish Review, Versus,* Fiddelhead Poetry Books, Villeneuve Publications and the author; for Lazar Sarna to The Porcupine's Quill and the author; for F.R. Scott to McClelland and Stewart, The Canadian Publishers, Blackfish Press and the author; for Daniel Sloate to Guernica Editions and the author; for David Solway to the Mansfield Book Mart, *Canadian Literature, CVII,* Valley/Mosaic Press, New Delta, Signal Editions and the author; for Richard Sommer to New Delta and the author; for Ben Soo to The Muses' Company and the author; for Ruth Taylor to The Muses' Company and the author; for Carole L. Ten Brink to *Poets On, Montreal Writers' Forum,* Bonsecours Editions and the author; for Joan Thornton-McLeod to *The Fiddlehead, Canadian Literature* and the author; for Peter Van Toorn to *Montreal Review, Montreal Writers' Forum, CrossCountry* and the author; for Jeremy Walker to DC Books and the author; for Paddy Webb to *The New Yorker, The McGill Journal of Education* and the author; for Jerry Wexler to the author; for Shulamis Yelin to The Reconstructionist Press and the author; for Noah Zacharin to *Scrivener* and the author.